A Straightforward Guide to

HEALTHCARE LAW

FOR PATIENTS, CARERS, AND PRACTITIONERS

Marc Cornock & Lindsay Giddings

Straightforward Publishing
www.straightforwardbooks.co.uk

Straightforward Guides
© Marc Cornock and Lindsay Giddings, First Edition, 2023

British cataloguing in Publication Data. A catalogue record for this book is available from the British Library.
978-1-80236-149-0

Printed by 4edge www.4edge.co.uk
Typesetting by Frabjous Books
Cover design by BW Studio Derby

Zoe & Jo,

I cannot thank you enough for all the support you have given to Sarah & I. Please accept this as a token of my gratitude.

Marc

To my mum, for being the best mum anybody could ever wish to have and for always being there for me. And to my husband, for supporting everything I want to do (even when it might be a bad idea). Thank you both and love you always.

Lindsay

CONTENTS

CONTENTS

CONTENTS

CONTENTS

PREFACE

Our aim in writing this book was to present what can be a complex subject in an accessible way, so that information is both easy to find and to understand.

This book is intended to be used by several different audiences: patients, those individuals who are currently interacting with health care practitioners; relatives and carers of those who are receiving care and/or treatment; health care practitioners and student health care practitioners who provide the care and treatment to the rest of us; and finally, those with an interest in healthcare law and rights.

We have written this book from the assumption that readers will not have any prior knowledge of healthcare law. The book includes all the areas necessary for each of the different audiences, yet we have kept the content as short as possible. Likewise, we have only included as much detail as is necessary to make the various points. This, we trust, will make the subject more user-friendly.

We hope you find it useful, informative and empowering.

Marc & Lindsay

ABOUT THE AUTHORS

Marc Cornock is a Senior Lecturer in Healthcare Law. He worked as a health care practitioner before moving into the education of health care practitioners. His interest in health care law developed during his time as a practitioner. Marc teaches and writes about health care law and how it affects practitioners and patients.

Marc has also written:

- Marc Cornock (2021) *Key Questions in Healthcare Law and Ethics* Sage
- Marc Cornock (2023) *Accountability and Professionalism in Nursing and Healthcare* Sage
- Marc Cornock (2023) *Consent: A Pocket Guide for Nursing and Health Care* Lantern Publishing

Marc's articles are available to download from: http://oro.open.ac.uk/view/person/mac755.html

Lindsay Giddings is a Lecturer in Social Work and is Programme Lead for Undergraduate and Apprenticeship Social Work. Before moving into academia, she worked as a social worker and senior practitioner, predominantly with children with disabilities. Lindsay is particularly interested in the social work workforce, and how they can be supported to be happy and effective practitioners.

Marc & Lindsay both work in the Faculty of Wellbeing, Education and Language Studies at The Open University.

ABBREVIATIONS

CPR	Cardio-pulmonary resuscitation
CQC	Care Quality Commission
DNACPR	Do not attempt cardio-pulmonaryresuscitation recommendation
DNAR	Do not attempt resuscitation
DoLS	Deprivation of Liberty Safeguards
DIY	Do it yourself
GP	General Practitioner
ICMA	Independent Mental Capacity Advocates
IMHA	Independent Mental Health Advocates
LPA	Lasting power of attorney
LPS	Liberty Protection Safeguards
NHS	National Health Service
PALS	Patient Advice and Liaison Service
UK	United Kingdom

INTRODUCTION

The purpose of this introduction is threefold: to give you an insight into how we have approached the writing and presentation of this book, the focus of the book, and, through a brief outline of each chapter, its structure.

Approach to writing and presentation

We have approached the writing and presentation of this book from the perspective of the patient. Therefore, it is written to, and refers to, you. You the patient. Most of the information within this book is relevant not just to patients but to their carers and healthcare practitioners as well. Therefore, we expect that carers and healthcare practitioners will see 'you' as their relative or their patient. However, where something has particular relevance for carers or healthcare practitioners, we have indicated this using the following symbols at the beginning of section and subsection headings:

⅄ for carers and also relatives
⚕ for healthcare practitioners

Where we have indicated that a section has particular relevance for a specific group, it doesn't mean that is has no relevance for anyone else, just that we think this is an area that the specified group will have a particular interest in.

In a similar manner, the information in this book applies to patients regardless of whether they are an adult or a child. However, there are times when there is a difference between how adult and child patients are treated and the principles that apply to each. In order to highlight these differences, we have included sections and subsections which explain and discuss the difference for child patients and so have used the word 'child' in the section or subsection heading to make it clear there is a difference.

A further aspect of our approach to writing this book that we would like to highlight is that you will find that we have adopted a conversational style, so that we directly address you in our writing, and you will find that we refer to 'you' a lot. Our conversational style of writing is meant to be informal, and this is because we wanted to move away from the dry academic texts that can be difficult to understand and which present a lot of information, so that finding the one thing you wanted can prove problematic. It is our hope that we have presented the information you need in a simple and relevant way, without overcomplicating or having too much information. Our writing mantra has been *keep it informative, relevant, simple and short.* Hopefully you will agree we achieved this.

A brief note on terms and terminology

Some words and terms used in law and healthcare, when taken out of context, could be offensive or patronising to some people. It is not our wish to offend anyone, and we have chosen our words carefully to try to avoid causing offence as well as minimising our use of those words that can be contentious. Where we have used a word that could be contentious, we have explained our reasoning. If you do come across a word that seems out of place, please accept that we are using it in a particular way for a particular purpose.

It is also worth noting that many excerpts from policy or legislation refer to 'he' and 'him', which may seem at best outdated, and at worst exclusionary. Until the mid-1850s, most legislation was written in a gender-neutral way. This changed with the introduction of the Interpretation Act 1850, which stated that *'words including the masculine gender shall include females'*. This was repeated in the Interpretation Act 1978, which still applies today. Since 2007, it has been government policy to use gender-neutral language in the writing of legislation. Throughout this book, gender-neutral language has been used unless for a specific purpose, or because there is reference to a specific source that has used gendered pronouns.

Focus of this book

This book is about healthcare law, how the delivery of healthcare is governed, and what this means for various groups of individuals, whether they are patients, carers, or healthcare practitioners. Our aim for this book is to explain how healthcare law interacts with patients, carers, and healthcare practitioners, and how it can support each of these to help patients achieve their healthcare needs.

Having said that the subject matter of this book is healthcare law and noting that the book's title is *Healthcare law for patients, carers and practitioners*, we can also say that the book is essentially concerned with the rights that patients have relating to their healthcare needs. This is because healthcare law exists to ensure that the rights of patients are protected in their healthcare interactions.

This also means that the law that governs and regulates healthcare practitioners needs to be discussed, as it is healthcare practitioners who assist patients in meeting their healthcare needs, and there are laws to ensure that healthcare practitioners work in a safe and competent way. Finally, we have discussed ethics and how they relate to healthcare law and patient rights.

However, rest assured that we have kept to our writing mantra and have kept the discussion of law and ethics *relevant, simple and short.*

If we were asked to give a one sentence answer to the question what is *Healthcare law for patients, carers and practitioners* about? we would say that is it about understanding the rights that patients have in relation to meeting their healthcare needs.

Structure of the book

As noted, when we discussed the focus above, this book is concerned with healthcare law and the rights of patients, and how patients, carers and healthcare practitioners can work together to achieve the patient's healthcare needs.

All of the chapters that follow this introduction are concerned with a specific aspect of meeting your healthcare needs. In reality, there will be overlap between the various stages that address your healthcare needs, and some may happen at the same time as others, so any attempt to separate them is an artificial one. Also, it is worth noting that we could have used different stages or put some of the issues and concepts we will discuss into a different chapter. That said, the following structure is the one that we feel is the most useful as well as being the more logical in terms of a progression through the healthcare process.

The structure of the book is as follows:

Rights (Chapter 1)

The focus of chapter 1 is on rights, what they are and how they arise, and how ethics and law are related to rights. We move on to consider healthcare rights and what rights a patient has. Healthcare rights are considered in relation to the NHS and its constitution. There is a discussion of the differences between rights, entitlements and wishes. Following this the chapter moves on to examine how a patient may be supported to enforce their healthcare rights. This is through a discussion of advocacy.

Engaging with healthcare (Chapter 2)

The focus of this chapter is on the patient and their interaction with the healthcare process. There is a discussion about the autonomy of patients, and whether a patient has a choice about who provides their care and treatment. This is followed by a consideration of what a healthcare practitioner is, why they are regulated and how they are regulated. The importance of knowing who is treating you is raised along with discussion of who can deliver healthcare to a patient. Because patient engagement with healthcare requires decisions to be made, there is discussion about the decision-making process and the role of both the patient and the healthcare practitioner in the decision-making process.

We also question whether a healthcare practitioner is obliged to provide care and treatment that a patient is requesting. The chapter concludes by considering the role of relatives and next of kin, as well as the role of chaperones.

Agreeing to treatment (Chapter 3)

The main focus of this chapter is on patient agreement to treatment. There is a brief discussion of what healthcare needs are, alongside treatment choice and treatment decisions, before examining the legal right to treatment. This leads into the main focus of the chapter which is an examination of consent in healthcare. We discuss the need for consent in healthcare before looking at what legally valid consent is, and what is necessary for consent from a patient to be considered legally valid.

The three components of legally valid consent are considered, including a discussion of how competence is assessed and how much information a patient needs to receive for the patient to be judged to be adequately informed.

The difference between assent and consent is explored, as well as terminology related to consent and competence.

The chapter considers the differences between the ability of an adult and a child patient to give their own consent, including a definition of what a child is from a legal perspective. The role of parents in a child's healthcare is examined, including their rights and responsibilities in relation to the child, and a discussion of what parental responsibility is and who may have it in relation to a child. There is consideration of conflicts that can arise between patients and healthcare practitioners when treatment choices are being made, as well as between parents and child patients, and healthcare practitioners and parents. Finally, the ways that a patient can give consent are outlined.

Refusing treatment (Chapter 4)

So far, we have discussed consent in this book in the positive, as a way of you giving permission for specific care and treatment offered to you by a healthcare practitioner. This chapter starts by recapping what consent is before considering whether consent is a single event or one that lasts continually after it has been given. Chapter 4 then moves on to examine the situation if you decide you don't want a specific treatment: the other side of the 'right to consent'. This includes a discussion of your right not to accept treatment that is offered to you, whether as an adult or a child patient, including self-discharge.

The chapter also looks at how a patient can change their mind about a treatment by looking at when a patient can withdraw their consent for a specific treatment.

Finally, chapter 4 considers the situation of healthcare practitioners who do not want to provide certain treatments and what their legal position is, through a consideration of conscientious objection.

When the patient lacks the capacity to consent for their own healthcare needs (Chapter 5)

In this chapter, we consider situations where a patient is not able to make their own decisions about their treatment options. This can be in emergency situations, or because the patient does not have the ability to make their own decisions dues to an illness.

It asks who can make a decision for a patient when the patient can't do so for themselves, and can a healthcare practitioner lawfully provide treatment to patients who lack the capacity to give their consent for that treatment?

The chapter begins by considering the reasons why a patient may lack the capacity to make their own treatment decisions, before examining the way in which treatment may lawfully be given to patients who lack capacity. This includes child and adult patients.

In relation to adult patients, this includes a discussion of advance decisions and lasting power of attorney. For both adult and child patients, it includes a discussion of the principle of necessity and best interests.

Following this is a consideration of how patients may have their liberty restricted, including through mental health legislation, which includes a discussion of the role of relatives, and also through the Deprivation of Liberty Safeguards.

Confidentiality (Chapter 6)

This chapter looks at confidentiality, also known in healthcare as clinical confidentiality. It starts by considering what confidentiality is and the need for confidentiality in healthcare. This leads into a discussion on how ethics and the law support confidentiality in healthcare and an examination of the duty of confidentiality that healthcare practitioners have.

This is followed by an examination of what confidential information is, how confidentiality can be maintained in healthcare and how confidential information may be lawfully shared and with whom. There is consideration of sharing information in the public interest and the sharing of information with relatives.

Chapter 6 then moves on to explore the actions a patient could take if their confidentiality was breached.

The difference between a child and an adult patient in relation to confidentiality is considered, as well as confidentiality after the death of a patient.

Health records and their purpose is discussed before an examination of how patients can access their own health records, as the accessing of health records by relatives.

Chapter 6 concludes by discussing visiting patients in hospital.

Decision-making around the end of life (Chapter 7)

Chapter 7 deals with some difficult issues centred around patient rights in relation to dying and death. We have approached the chapter so that issues that arise before death are discussed first, then the issues around death and dying itself, and finally those issues that occur after the death of a patient.

The issues we discuss in this chapter are resuscitation and do not attempt resuscitation orders, withholding and withdrawal of treatment, followed by suicide and euthanasia. We then move on to consider the definition of death, how death is certified and registering a death.

The chapter ends by examining organ donation.

Questioning healthcare (Chapter 8)

This chapter discusses the various aspects and ways of questioning healthcare. This includes how to raise your concerns when things go wrong, or you believe they have gone wrong or when things are not as you would want them. As well as raising concerns, the chapter considers whether you can expect someone to say sorry if a mistake has occurred as well as honesty and transparency from healthcare providers through the duty of candour and a healthcare practitioner's professional duty of candour.

Chapter 8 then moves on to consider complaints and how a complaint can be made, before analysing negligence, including what it is and how it is decided. The chapter ends by discussing the standard to which healthcare practitioners are held and how to report a concern about a particular healthcare practitioner to their regulatory body.

After chapter 8, there is a glossary of terms that are used in the book.

We have also included a resources section which includes various websites that may be useful if you wish to follow up on some of the services we mention that are available to patients and carers in the different chapters.

Although we have written this book so that it follows a healthcare journey the typical patient may take through the healthcare system, it does not have to be read in a set order and each chapter is self-contained (if information in another chapter is needed this will be highlighted). The contents page and the summary of each chapter above should allow you to find where the information you want is being discussed so that you can jump straight to that if you are looking for something specific.

CHAPTER 1

RIGHTS

The focus of chapter 1 is on rights, what they are and how they arise, and how ethics and law are related to rights. We move on to consider healthcare rights and what rights a patient has. Healthcare rights are considered in relation to the NHS and its constitution. There is a discussion of the differences between rights, entitlements and wishes. Following this the chapter moves on to examine how a patient may be supported to enforce their healthcare rights. This is through a discussion of advocacy.

Exploring what is meant by rights

How many times have you heard someone say, or even said yourself, 'it's my right, I can do X'? Probably quite a few, yet what is meant when someone says they have a right to do X?

Rights are generally referred to as the ability or freedom to do something or to have something, without being stopped from doing it or prevented from having it. If you have a right but someone else can stop you from exercising that right, then you don't really have that right as it is subject to someone else allowing you to enjoy it. For instance, suppose Marc, one of the writers, believes he has the right to watch the Six Nations rugby matches uninterrupted by any member of his family (quite a nice right to have!) Is this a real right? Probably not, as it is easy to see that he could be interrupted by regular family life, and it is subject to his family members not interrupting him and allowing him to watch uninterrupted.

1. RIGHTS

Where one person has a right, others have an obligation to uphold this right. So, for Marc, if he has the right to watch the Six Nations rugby matches uninterrupted, his other family members would be obliged not to interrupt him.

A key element of a right is being able to enforce that right. Could Marc enforce his rugby watching right and enforce the obligation of other family members to allow him to watch uninterrupted? Again, highly unlikely. If all his family members got together and decide they wanted to watch the match with him and check what was going on in the game, it is difficult to see how he could enforce his 'right'.

Rights need the support of the law to be enforceable. If a right is set out in law, then the individual who feels their right has been abused can go to court to have their right enforced, otherwise it is not a right but an *aspiration*. Could you see Marc being able to use the courts to enforce his rugby watching desires successfully? No, neither can Marc's family members. Marc has an aspiration to watch the rugby matches uninterrupted but not a legally enforceable right!

The rights which we all have usually arise from an ethical belief that something needs protecting, for instance the right to be free from slavery or forced labour.

Human rights

Sometimes a set of rights, often referred to as basic rights or universal human rights, are seen as needing protecting. The United Kingdom has a long history of acknowledging the rights and freedoms of individuals. This can be traced back to 1215 and the Magna Carta which first recognised that citizens had their own rights. In 1689 the English Bill of Rights clarified what the rights of a citizen were and extended those rights, for instance the right not to be tortured.

What can be classed as 'modern' human rights originate

from the Universal Declaration of Human Rights in 1948. This Declaration set out what every human, regardless of their country of origin or where they live, has a right to and the freedoms they can expect.

The 1948 Declaration resulted in the European Convention on Human Rights in 1950. The United Kingdom signed the Convention in 1951 and it came into force in 1953. The difference between the declaration of 1948 and the 1950 Convention is that the Convention could be used in the European Court of Human Rights (a court that is held in Strasbourg) to enforce a right.

Between 1951 and 1998, several specific laws came into force which protected specific rights. These included the Sex Discrimination Act 1975 (which made discrimination based on a person's gender illegal), the Race Relations Act 1976 (which made discrimination based on someone's race illegal) and the Disability Act 1995 (which made discrimination based on someone's disability illegal).

The Human Rights Act 1998 took the principles of the European Convention on Human Rights 1950 and put them into the law of the United Kingdom. This means that a person who wants to enforce one of their rights can do so in a court in the United Kingdom.

Since the introduction of the Human Rights Act 1998, other pieces of legislation have extended or clarified the law on an individual's rights. An example would be the Equality Act 2010 which replaced over 100 separate pieces of legislation to advance and protect the rights of all.

Some of the rights and freedoms protected in the law of the United Kingdom include:

- The right to life
- Freedom from torture
- Freedom from slavery and forced labour
- The right to liberty and security

- The right to a fair trial
- The right to respect for privacy and family life
- Freedom of thought, conscience and religion
- Freedom of expression

In brief, a right is the right or freedom to do something or be protected from something that originates in ethical beliefs and is given substance and protected by the law.

Ethics

We are discussing ethics because the rights that exist come from the ethical beliefs that exist in a given country or society. Rights come from how individuals are viewed and what conduct is expected of them, and what conduct an individual can expect from others. Ethics can be said to be concerned with the rules of conduct and duty that define how individuals behave toward each other.

There are several ethical theories that exist to explain how someone should behave toward another person. Two of the predominant traditional ethical theories are consequentialism and deontology.

Consequentialism is concerned with the consequence of an action. Those actions where the consequence results in good rather than harm are seen as more desirable than those which result in harm. The greater the good that results as a consequence of an action, the more desirable that action is.

Deontology is concerned with doing duty. This ethical theory is based on individuals performing certain actions because they are duty bound to do so. 'Good' or 'bad' for someone who follows deontology is concerned with whether someone acts or not. Failing to act when there is a duty to do so is bad.

Both consequentialism and deontology can be problematic when applied to healthcare. Consequentialism, because it cannot always be known if an action will result in a good or harmful outcome, for instance if a healthcare practitioner's intentions were good but harm results because of their action; is this a good or bad action? Whereas deontology can be seen as being emotionless because the person acts not out of a desire to help but because they are duty bound to do so.

Modern healthcare ethics have moved away from the traditional ethical theories and adopt a professional ethics or values ethics approach. The professional ethics approach uses a framework of principles to adopt when working with patients and providing healthcare to meet the needs of patients.

These principles are:

- Autonomy
- Beneficence
- Justice
- Non-maleficence

Autonomy is about the right to make one's own decision and not having decisions made by others, or in healthcare not having treatments forced upon you.

Beneficence is concerned with others doing things for your good and your benefit.

Justice is connected to fairness. In some ways, it is about treating a patient according to the needs they have rather than, say, their ability to pay, or because they are the most vocal in asking for a treatment.

Non-maleficence is primarily concerned with ensuring that healthcare practitioners do not harm their patients. An example would be that a healthcare practitioner knows the risk associated with giving a particular patient a specific treatment and only proceeds where the risk of not acting outweighs the potential for harm through acting.

Individually, each of the four principles protects patient rights. Together, these four principles can be said to underpin healthcare law and thus the rights that can be legally enforced by an individual in relation to their healthcare needs and the healthcare they receive. These ethical principles also underpin the regulation that governs how healthcare practitioners are expected to work and interact with their patients. For instance, the ethical principle of autonomy requires that healthcare practitioners accept that the patient has the right to determine what happens to their body. This has not always been the case, as you will see when consent is discussed in chapter 3 *Agreeing to treatment*.

Law

Aside from the fact that it is in the title of this book, we need to talk about the law because it is the law that protects the rights that you have as a patient receiving healthcare.

The law can be thought of as a formal set of rules; rules that are thought of as so important that breaking the rules can result in some form of punishment. As an example, in the UK there is an unwritten rule that if a queue exists, you join the back of the queue. However, this is not a law, and you cannot be taken to court and punished if you don't join the back of the queue. In the UK, it is more of a custom or form of politeness to join the back of a queue.

Now, if you had punched the person at the front of the queue so that you could take their place, this would be something that could result in you appearing in court and being punished, maybe with a fine or a community order. This is because there is a rule in place not to punch other people – a rule that is so important it has the weight of the law behind it.

All the rules that exist in a particular country that can be enforced in the courts are the law for that country.

Having a law that protects an ethical value such as autonomy, as with the law on consent, is the mechanism whereby ethical principles are formally embedded and protected. It is the law in its widest sense that gives substance to the ethical values that are considered important in any society and underpin the rights that individuals have.

Types of law

There are two main types of law: legislation and common law. Legislation refers to law that is made by or on behalf of parliament, such as Acts of Parliament and statutory instruments, whereas common law refers to law that is based on the judgments made in cases that come before the courts and are developed over a number of years. If legislation and common law are in conflict, legislation will prevail. As an example, for many years the law on consent was based on common law through cases where the court was asked to judge if a patient was able to give their own consent. Now, the Mental Capacity Act 2005 provides guidance on consent, particularly the ability of patients to give their own consent. Although the law in the cases still exists, the Mental Capacity Act 2005 is the primary source for this area of law.

As laws do not go 'out of date' and exist until they are removed, many of the laws that exist today originated many years ago. For instance, the law regarding assaulting someone is in part from an Act of 1861 (the Offences Against the Person Act 1861) that is still in force today.

Because of the complexity of finding and understanding the law, it can be difficult to know what the law says about any specific aspect of life. Law can be categorised according to the aspect of society that it deals with. For instance, the law that deals with buying and selling houses is known as property law, that which deals with crime is criminal law, and that which deals with agreements between individuals and organisations is contract law.

Healthcare law

Healthcare law is a relatively new area of law in the legal field, and like many areas of law it 'borrows' from many other areas of law. A large part of healthcare law is concerned with an area of law called 'tort'. Tort law is concerned with when one person or organisation wrongs another and the remedies that can be used. Other areas of law that are used in healthcare law are concerned with what public bodies do, and others with how healthcare and healthcare practitioners are regulated.

Healthcare law is important because it is the area of law that supports patient healthcare rights and enforces the obligations that others, such as healthcare practitioners, have to a patient. It is healthcare law that governs the relationship between healthcare practitioner and patient and ensures that the needs of the patient are paramount in that relationship.

Whether you are a patient or a healthcare practitioner you may be asking yourself what laws do you need to be aware of? Throughout this book, relevant laws will be explored and pointed out to you – we believe these are the ones you need to know about. They will be the ones that relate to patient rights.

Rights in healthcare

Having discussed what a right is and how rights relate to ethical principles and are underpinned by the law so that they can be enforced, it is time to look at what healthcare rights you actually have.

We think this may come as a bit of a surprise, so bear with us on this one. You only really have one healthcare right as a matter of course. This is the right to be registered with a general practitioner (GP).

Now, although you have the right to register with one GP, you cannot register with the GP of your choice as a right. What the right to be registered with a GP means, is that you can approach a GP practice and ask to be registered with them. If they are unable to register you, perhaps because their practice list is full, a GP will be found for you to register with.

Once you have registered with a GP, your right has been fulfilled. You cannot register with a second GP. You can transfer your registration from one GP to another but cannot register with two at the same time. This means that if you are away from home and need to see a GP, you need to request emergency treatment from a local GP surgery. This is permitted for up to 14 days. You can also have a temporary registration with another GP if you are going to be away from home for over 24 hours but less than three months.

The reason we say that you only have the right to be registered with a GP is because a GP acts as a gatekeeper to most healthcare services, apart from emergency care such as that provided in an emergency department when you can turn up and ask to be seen or if you are taken by ambulance. Services such as dental and optician type services, to whom you can self-refer, are also excluded from the need to see a GP first.

It is the GP who makes the decision as to whether you should access other parts of the healthcare system. When we say healthcare system, we are talking about the National Health Service (NHS). This means that if the GP does not think that you need the services of another healthcare practitioner, for instance a hospital consultant, you will not be able to access that. In chapter 2 *Engaging with healthcare,* we discuss healthcare decision-making and what you can do if do not agree with your healthcare practitioner.

The NHS Constitution and Patient's Charter

When discussing healthcare rights, it is very common for both patients and healthcare practitioners to believe that patients have more enforceable rights than they actually have. Part of the reason that patients and others believe that there are more healthcare rights than actually exist is because of initiatives such as the NHS Constitution and the Patient's Charter (Department of Health 1991).

Each of the 4 nations of the United Kingdom has its own NHS. Referring to the NHS Constitution for England (Department of Health and Social Care 2021) as an example, it is possible to see that patient rights are mentioned, and there is even a section titled *'Patients and the public: your rights and the NHS pledges to you'*. This can give the impression that a lot of rights exist. However, whilst some of the rights exist, others are, as the title refers to, a pledge or an intention on behalf of the NHS, but not an enforceable right. It is something the NHS would like to do or offer, but one that it may not always achieve.

One of the pledges in the NHS Constitution for England is to receive treatment free of charge. Now, this is generally true but not always the case. For instance, some people must pay prescription charges or pay for dental treatment. Other treatments, such as that provided in an emergency department, are provided free of charge. So, you can see that not all services provided by the NHS are free of charge, despite the pledge in the NHS Constitution.

So, whilst treatment may be free of charge it is not a legally enforceable right as there may be occasions when you are expected to pay. Indeed, the NHS constitution for England does acknowledge this as it states that patients *'have the right to receive NHS services free of charge, apart from certain limited exceptions sanctioned by Parliament'* (it is Parliament which sets the requirement for prescription fees etc).

As an aside, prescriptions issued with the NHS are free in Northern Ireland, Scotland and Wales. This includes prescriptions issued by NHS General Practitioners.

However, in England prescriptions issued by a GP are not

free unless you are in an exempt category. The reason for this lies with the politics of healthcare in the individual countries. It can be rather frustrating and lead to some anomalies. For instance, if you are registered with a GP in England but live in Scotland or Wales you can apply for an entitlement card which allows you to have your prescription dispensed in Scotland or Wales and thus not have to pay for it.

Similarly, the Patient's Charter (Department of Health 1991), which was originally published in 1991, set out a number of rights and standards that patients could expect. For instance, some of the rights and standards relate to waiting times for ambulance response or the time limit within which a patient wating in an emergency department should be seen. However, as with the NHS Constitution, these are aspirations of the NHS rather than legally enforceable rights.

With documents such as these it is easy to see why there is confusion about what rights a patient can expect during their healthcare interactions.

Healthcare wishes, healthcare entitlements or healthcare rights

Let's consider the difference between a healthcare wish, a healthcare entitlement, and a healthcare right.

A healthcare wish is something that you may want to happen. You may want to receive your treatment during the summer when the right season is over. You can wish for it but there is no guarantee that it will happen then, and no right to have treatment when you want.

A healthcare expectation is something that you and others can expect to happen but not something that is guaranteed or that you can legally enforce. An example of a healthcare expectation is that the treatment you receive will resolve your condition. You may also wish this, but a healthcare expectation raises a wish to something that you can expect to happen. Expect – but not guarantee, and not enforce. This is because with any treatment there are factors which may mean that treatment which works for one patient may not work for you, despite the best efforts of everyone involved.

A healthcare right is one that you can legally enforce. It is a step on from a healthcare expectation in that as well as expecting it to happen, you can legally enforce it if it doesn't. Registering with a GP is the example we have used in this chapter as a legally enforceable healthcare right.

Looking at healthcare wishes, expectations and rights using the GP as an example:

You may *wish* that your GP is Dr X. You can ask but not demand this as Dr X's patient list may be full.

You may *expect* to see a GP today. Whilst this may be likely, it is not guaranteed and you may find that when you call for an appointment you are triaged, that is your condition is rated in terms of severity, and you are given an appointment appropriate for you clinical need, which may not be today.

You may need to register with a GP. As this is a *right*, if you yourself cannot find a GP willing to allow you to register, one will be found for you.

When discussing your right to be registered with a GP earlier in this chapter, it was noted that the reason that this right exists is because the GP acts as a gatekeeper to the rest of the NHS. It is the GP who refers you as a patient to other NHS services and other NHS healthcare practitioners.

Without being referred you will not be able to access those other NHS services. This is an important point because it is when your GP refers you to other NHS services or other NHS healthcare practitioners that your other healthcare rights start to come into play. Essentially, your other healthcare rights exists when you have been referred for investigation or treatment.

One reason why the GP acts as gatekeeper and your other

healthcare rights do not exist until you are referred is to stop you having the legal right to demand treatment that is unwarranted and going to court to enforce that. This can be related to the ethical value of justice as it prevents resources being used unnecessarily.

Once you have been accepted for treatment in the NHS you can now enforce rights that you previously did not have.

In this book we will discuss the actual rights that you have once you have been referred for treatment or when you are receiving treatment as the appropriate points in later chapters. As an example, and a little teaser, these rights include the right to privacy (discussed in chapter 6 *Confidentiality*), and the right to exercise autonomy in either agreeing to treatment (discussed in chapter 3 *Agreeing to treatment*) or refusing treatment (discussed in chapter 4 *Refusing treatment*).

Advocacy in healthcare

It may seem a bit odd have a section on advocacy in healthcare in a chapter on rights but let us explain our thinking. We have seen in this chapter so far that as a patient you have certain rights. Also, we demonstrated that for these to be actual rights, as opposed to expectations, they need to be enforceable. Now, because of your condition, your needs or even something else such as your personality, you may not be able to enforce these rights yourself or even know that you have them. This is where advocacy and advocates come into play.

Advocacy is concerned with acting on behalf of someone who is unable to act for themselves. According to the Shorter Oxford English Dictionary advocacy is '*pleading in support of*', and an advocate is '*a person who pleads, intercedes, or speaks for another*' (Stevenson 2007).

Traditionally an advocate was a lawyer who represents their client in court, speaking on their behalf. The lawyer has the necessary knowledge and skills to be able to present their client's case to the best advantage for the client. In healthcare, advocacy fulfils the same function. It is when someone supports and speaks up for or on behalf of a patient in accessing and using healthcare services, to ensure that the patient's rights are met.

Advocates can support patients in a number of ways to ensure that the patient's voice is heard. These may include:

- Listening to you to understand what is important to you and what it is you want
- Discussing your concerns about your condition or any proposed or planned treatment
- Helping you understand what support there is in helping you manage your condition
- Assisting you in exploring the options available to you
- Helping you to find the information that you need to make a decision
- Being with you when you have discussions with healthcare practitioners
- Supporting you during any appointments and meetings you have
- Helping you to remember any information and discussion during your appointments
- Assisting you to understand the outcome of any appointments and meetings
- Helping you to consider what you want from your treatment and the pros and cons of any specific treatment
- Challenging any decisions that are made about you that you do not agree with
- Aiding you in communicating your wishes and feelings

There are many reasons why a patient may need an advocate, for instance, the patient may:

- be unconscious, and so unable to participate in their healthcare
- not have the mental capacity to understand what is happening, and so not able to fully engage in their healthcare decision making
- be confused by what is being said to them about their diagnosis or treatment options, and need simpler explanations or for a written record
- be lacking in confidence to make their own decision
- be fearful of healthcare practitioners
- consider that healthcare practitioners know what is right and so whatever they say is right
- not know how to speak up for themselves

A patient may need or want an advocate for all their appointments or interactions with healthcare practitioners. They may also only want or need an advocate at specific times, or for specific reasons.

Choosing an advocate

Anyone can be an advocate. It is about supporting a patient to access and use healthcare and obtaining the right care and treatment at the right time according to the patient's needs. Therefore, anyone who is able to provide that support to the patient can act as their advocate. This could be a relative or a friend. It is worth noting that a carer who is paid by a local council or social services to provide care for you is usually not allowed to be an advocate.

When considering who you want as your advocate, it needs to be someone that you trust to act on your behalf and not put forward their own agenda or wishes.

Healthcare practitioners can act as a patient advocate. However, they need to ensure that they separate their role as patient advocate from their role in treating the patient.

Advocacy services

There are a number of formal ways of having an advocate in healthcare settings.

The Mental Health Act 2007 introduced Independent Mental Health Advocates (IMHAs) for those patients who are subject to the provisions of the Mental Health Act 1983. IMHAs are specifically trained for their role, which includes assisting patients to understand what their rights are, the restrictions they are subject to, and how they can participate in their treatment and any decision-making.

As well as introducing Independent Mental Health Advocates, the Mental Health Act 2007 also made it a requirement that patients who would benefit from the services of an IMHA should be told that help is available to them from an IMHA and how they can access that help.

Under the provisions of the Mental Capacity Act 2005, Independent Mental Capacity Advocates (ICMAs) were introduced for those patients who are not able to make decisions for themselves, and who do not have anyone who is able act as an advisor and support them in the decision making about their care and treatment.

The Care Act 2014 puts an obligation on local councils to have an independent advocacy service for individuals who are not able to advocate for themselves in relation to their care needs. It is designed for those individuals who do not have a relative or friend or carer who is able to support them. The service is also available to carers who do not have the support of someone else.

The advocacy under the Care Act 2014 is limited to supporting you in relation to your care and support or safeguarding needs such as local authority assessments and care planning. It does not extend to advocacy for healthcare needs. You are entitled to independent advocacy under the Care Act 2014 so long as you do not have anybody else who can support you, and you have significant difficulties in being involved in an assessment of your needs or plan for your care.

There is also an advocacy service known as the NHS Complaints Advocacy who provide advocacy to patients and other individuals who are making a complaint, or thinking of making a complaint, in relation to health services. Although the advocacy service has NHS in its title, it is independent of the NHS and covers complaints about NHS services that are provided in private hospitals and clinics.

All of the advocacy services above are free to the user. There is no obligation on a patient to use any of these advocacy services. And if a patient does use one, they can decide to stop using them at any time. Patients are also entitled to use an advocate of their choosing instead of any of the formal advocacy services.

Advocacy and the child patient

Where the patient is a child, it is expected that the parent or another person with parental responsibility, if there is one, will act as the child's advocate. This is because the parent is the person who is there to represent the child and their best interests.

It is only when the parent is unable to act for the child would another advocate be sought to represent the child, or if it considered that the parent is not acting in the child's best interests.

◙ Healthcare practitioners as advocates

If you are a healthcare practitioner, you may find that one of the duties you are expected to follow in your code of conduct is related to advocacy. For instance, the Nursing and Midwifery Council requires healthcare practitioners who are registered with it to act as advocates for their patients. It specifically states this in the code of conduct it issues to all its registrants, noting that healthcare practitioners should 'act as advocates for the vulnerable' (Nursing and Midwifery Council 2018 at paragraph 3.4).

If you do not have an advocate

If you feel that you need an advocate but don't have one at present, you can request one using any of the formal routes just discussed, for example, an IMCA or IMHA, if you qualify. Alternatively, if you do not qualify, you can approach your local council's social services department and ask if they are able to assist you.

There are also charities that provide help to people who need an advocate. It can be worth checking the charities in your local area and asking if they have advocates able to assist you. Some national advocacy services are included in the *Resources* section at the end of the book.

Advocates attending appointments

An advocate can support you before, during and after any interaction you have with healthcare practitioners. This means that they can attend your appointments with you if you wish.

Advocacy and interpreters

Because the role of an advocate is to support you, there is a difference between having an advocate and an interpreter. Whilst a patient may need an interpreter to assist them in their healthcare interactions, the role of the interpreter is to faithfully interpret the communication between the patient and healthcare practitioner. They are not there to support the patient or assist them in their decision-making. That is the role of the advocate. Therefore, some patients may need an advocate and an interpreter.

Advocates and decision-making

Except in very limited situations, which will be discussed later, an advocate should not make a decision for you, nor should they put their views or opinions forward. They should not act without your permission to do so and any action they take should be limited to what you want them to do. Their role is to support you to make your own decisions based on the information you require and to ensure your voice is heard.

An advocate can put forward your views and decisions when you are unable to do this for yourself, but it should be *your* view and *your* decision they are communicating.

Disagreeing with your advocate

There should not be a situation where you need to disagree with your advocate. The advocate is there to support you and present your concerns and your viewpoints when you are not able to do this yourself.

If there is a situation where the advocate is doing something that you do not want them to do or is trying to persuade you to agree to a particular course of action, the person acting as advocate is not doing their role properly. They have in fact stepped outside of their role as your advocate into something entirely different.

Whenever you feel that there is a need for you to disagree with their advice, stop and consider what role the advocate is assuming and whether this is something that is working for you. Your advocate works for you, according to your needs and your wishes. They act for you; you do not act for them or according to what they think is right.

CHAPTER 2

ENGAGING WITH HEALTHCARE

The focus of this chapter is on the patient and their interaction with the healthcare process. There is a discussion about the autonomy of patients, and whether a patient has a choice about who provides their care and treatment. This is followed by a consideration of what a healthcare practitioner is, why they are regulated and how they are regulated. The importance of knowing who is treating you is raised along with a discussion of who can deliver healthcare to a patient. Because patient engagement with healthcare requires decisions to be made, there is discussion about the decision-making process and the role of both the patient and the healthcare practitioner in the decision-making process.

We also question whether a healthcare practitioner is obliged to provide care and treatment that a patient is requesting. The chapter concludes by considering the role of relatives and next of kin, as well as the role of chaperones.

Autonomy in healthcare

We first raised the concept of autonomy when discussing ethics in chapter 1, *Rights*, where it was noted that it was one of the principles associated with healthcare ethics. In chapter 1, it was stated that '*autonomy is about the right to make one's own decision and not having decisions made by others, or in healthcare not having treatments forced upon you*'.

Autonomy is a part of self-determination, which is concerned with the ability of an individual to make their own decisions and to control their own life and life choices. The word autonomy refers to being self-ruling.

To exercise autonomy and to be autonomous, you have to feel that you have a real choice and that you have free will to make a decision to accept or reject something. If you make a decision because someone has influenced you to make that decision, you have not been truly autonomous. If, however, you make a decision because it is something you have considered and you are aware that you can make any choice you wish, you are being autonomous. By making an autonomous decision and not letting others make decisions for you, unless you decide to let someone make a decision for you knowing that it is your choice to do so, you are determining your life choices, and exercising self-determination.

The ability of a patient to exercise their ethical right to self-determination when considering their healthcare needs is legally enshrined in consent. Consent is the legal right of a patient to make their own healthcare decisions and can be said to be legal recognition of the importance of the ethical right to self-determination. Because it is such an important aspect of treatment and making decisions about treatment choices, consent will be more fully considered in chapter 3 *Agreeing to treatment*.

In the healthcare context it can be easier to see what autonomy means by considering the situation if a patient were *not* allowed to be autonomous. As we will see in chapter 5 *When the patient lacks the capacity to consent for their own healthcare needs*, there are times when a patient is unable to be autonomous and to make their own decisions. If a patient is not making their own healthcare decisions, then someone else needs to make them. However, there are situations when a patient is able to make their own healthcare decisions but is not allowed to do so.

Because patients need healthcare practitioners to assist them in meeting their healthcare needs, and it is the healthcare practitioner who has the skills and knowledge, there is nearly always a power imbalance in the relationship between patient and healthcare practitioner, with the patient having the lesser power. Most healthcare practitioners recognise this imbalance of power and work with the patient, as we will see later in this chapter, to ensure that patients can exercise their autonomy and make their own treatment decisions. However, there are some healthcare practitioners who do not always recognise that the patient is a partner in meeting their healthcare needs. Instead of working in partnership with the patient, they take a paternalistic approach and make decisions for the patient. Instead of providing the patient with the information they need to make a decision, they might instead tell the patient that they need a certain treatment and not allow the patient to form their own opinion.

Being told that treatment X is your only option and that you have to have it does not allow you to be autonomous because it is not a decision based on a free choice. Paternalism by a healthcare practitioner is the opposite of a patient exercising their autonomy, as the healthcare practitioner is dominating the decision-making process. In exercising their autonomy, a patient has the right to ignore what a healthcare practitioner advises them to do, and to even make a decision that the healthcare practitioner does not agree with or even considers to be inappropriate.

The paternalistic healthcare practitioner does not allow a patient to make a decision that they, the healthcare practitioner, does not agree with. The healthcare practitioner supporting the patient's right to make an autonomous decision does.

Although paternalism is painted as being a negative aspect of healthcare in the discussion above, there is a place for paternalism in healthcare. The expertise of the healthcare practitioner can be crucial to ensuring that a patient's healthcare needs are met by making decisions on behalf of the patient. However, a healthcare practitioner should only make decisions for patients who lack autonomy. When patients are unable to make their own decisions, that is when they are said to lack autonomy.

Autonomy, then, is the ability of a patient to make their own decisions about their own healthcare needs, even when others disagree with the choices they are making. It is a legal right through the legal principle of consent and can be enforced.

Although patients have the right to exercise autonomy in their own healthcare decision-making, they need individuals who can assist them in meeting their healthcare needs and to provide the treatment they need. These individuals are healthcare practitioners and are discussed in the next section.

Healthcare practitioners

There are various types of healthcare practitioner who may assist you in meeting your healthcare needs. Some of these healthcare practitioners include:

- Art therapists
- Chiropodists
- Dieticians
- Doctors
- Midwives
- Nurses
- Occupational therapists
- Paramedics
- Physiotherapists
- Psychologists
- Radiographers
- Speech and language therapists

What they all have is common is that they assist and support patients in achieving their healthcare needs, albeit they do so in different ways.

Aside from their different specialities, healthcare practitioners can be categorised into two main groups: those who are registered, and those who are unregistered. A registered healthcare practitioner will have completed a set period of education and passed certain competencies necessary for entry to the register of the professional group they are joining. Once entered onto the register, they will have to maintain their professional competence and demonstrate that they have done so on a regular basis. They will be subject to an ethical code of conduct and be required to maintain a standard of practice.

We will discuss the regulation of healthcare practitioners and the standard to which they are held and their liability in chapter 8 *Questioning healthcare*. For now, we will just say that a registered healthcare practitioner could be referred to their regulatory body for a fitness to practise investigation if they do not maintain their standards. This might be because they fail to maintain their competence, if they breach their code of conduct, or if their practice is deemed to fall below the required standards. A fitness to practise investigation can have a number of outcomes, ranging from no further action through to the practitioner being removed from the register. If this happens, they would be unable to work in a role that requires registration.

All of the healthcare practitioners in the list above are registered practitioners. Unregistered practitioners include most students who are training to join their respective registers and support workers.

The difference between a registered and unregistered healthcare practitioner is that the former have demonstrated their ability to reach and maintain a set level of competence and that they can work at a given standard of practice, whilst unregistered healthcare practitioners have not. Generally, unregistered healthcare practitioners work under the supervision of a registered healthcare practitioner. This is to increase patient safety, because registered healthcare practitioners are subject to oversight by a healthcare practitioner regulator and unregistered healthcare practitioners are not.

Healthcare practitioner titles

In order to provide protection to the public and to patients from healthcare practitioners who have not met their standards, the healthcare practitioner regulators restrict the use of certain titles to those who are on their respective registers. These titles are known as protected titles. If someone were to use a protected title without being on the relevant register, they would be committing a criminal offence, and if convicted they could be subject to an unlimited fine.

Some of the protected titles describe the role that the healthcare practitioner has, for instance dietician, midwife and paramedic are all protected titles. To be able to use the title dietician or paramedic, the healthcare practitioner has to be registered with the Health and Care Professions Council. To use the title midwife, the healthcare practitioner has to be registered with the Nursing & Midwifery Council.

Some of the titles that are protected are not the usual titles that you may expect. For instance, 'doctor' and 'nurse' are not protected titles. Thus, it is not a criminal offence for anyone to call themselves a nurse or a doctor. What is protected for each of these two practitioner groups is a different title. For doctors this is 'registered medical practitioner', and for nurses it is 'registered nurse'.

There are several reasons why some titles are not protected but an alternative is. Some of these reasons are historical and others are related to the fact that there are other groups of individuals who have a valid claim to use the title and protecting it would cause more problems than it would solve. For example, certain academics use the title doctor when they achieve a higher degree, and there are other groups who use the title nurse other than healthcare practitioners, such as veterinary nurses and nursery nurses.

Although the protected titles are registered medical practitioner and registered nurse, in this book we will use the familiar doctor and nurse.

The aim behind protecting a specific title for a specified group of healthcare practitioners is so that patients know that the person treating them is registered and thus has achieved the standard that is required for registration. The next section further explains why you might want to know who is treating you.

Who can provide healthcare treatment

Now, you may be reading this thinking 'obviously healthcare treatment has to be provided by a healthcare practitioner'. It seems so obvious that you wonder why we are even asking the question. Well, we ask because we wanted to let you know that anyone can provide healthcare treatment. It does not have to be a healthcare practitioner. Neither Lindsay nor Marc are currently healthcare practitioners but either of them could lawfully provide healthcare to you or anyone else without fear of prosecution.

Now we say that, but there are two big caveats.

The first caveat is that the person offering to treat you cannot claim to be something that they are not. They should not lie to you or let you believe something they know is untrue. In particular, they should not claim to be a registered healthcare practitioner if they are not. As you will have seen in the previous section, there are two types of healthcare practitioner; those who are registered and those who are not. Being registered brings with it certain entitlements and obligations as described above. One entitlement is that they have their name entered onto a register of similar healthcare practitioners, and they are obliged to maintain a certain standard of practice.

Because registration allows patients to know that a healthcare practitioner has reached a certain standard of practice, anyone who falsely claims to be registered is committing a criminal offence and can receive an unlimited fine or imprisonment. The person attempting to provide treatment should also not claim that they have qualifications that they do not have.

The second caveat is that there are some specific areas of healthcare practice that are legally restricted and can only be performed by specific registered healthcare practitioners.

These restricted areas of healthcare practice and the legislation that imposes the restriction are:

- Abortion may only be authorised and supervised by doctors (Abortion Act 1967)
- Attending to a woman in childbirth is restricted to doctors or midwives, unless it is an emergency, or it is a student doctor or midwife as part of their training (The Nursing and Midwifery Order 2001)
- Certifying death can only be undertaken by doctors (Births and Deaths Registration Act 1953)
- Certifying a sick note, now formally called a fit note, is limited to doctors and certain other registered healthcare practitioners such as nurses, occupational therapists, pharmacists, and physiotherapists (The Social Security (Medical Evidence) and Statutory Sick Pay (Medical Evidence) (Amendment) (No. 2) Regulations 2022)
- Female genital mutilation is restricted to doctors unless it is need as part of the labour or birth of a child when a midwife may perform it (Female Genital Mutilation Act 2003)
- Tattooing someone under 18 may only be undertaken by a doctor (Tattooing of Minors Act 1969)

If anyone else were to undertake the areas of healthcare practice in the bulleted list, they could be charged with committing a criminal offence.

As long as neither Lindsay nor Marc describe themselves as registered healthcare practitioners and do not undertake any of the healthcare practices that are restricted to registered healthcare practitioners, there is nothing to legally stop them treating you, whether that treatment is for a headache, small cut on your hand or even amputating your hand because it is infected.

Of course, you need to give us permission to treat you, so that should stop either of us practising healthcare in the near future. But it is a sobering thought that so few areas of healthcare practice are limited to registered healthcare practitioners, which is why it is important that you know who is treating you as discussed earlier in this chapter, and why healthcare practitioners are regulated. This enables you to be assured of their level of training and competence.

Healthcare decision-making

The purpose of healthcare decision-making is to meet your healthcare needs by ensuring that you receive the care and treatment that is appropriate for your condition and that you agree to receive.

Healthcare decision-making is a process that has several stages to it. Some of these stages include:

- Identifying the healthcare need or issue
- Determining what you want to achieve
- Considering various treatment options
- Deciding upon a particular course of action

There are different roles that you and the healthcare practitioner take in the decision-making process. For instance, the healthcare practitioner might have to assess your healthcare need(s), investigate your condition, reach a diagnosis or decide upon appropriate treatment options that they will offer to you, along with an explanation of the benefits and possible complications of any treatment. Your role includes ensuring that you inform the healthcare practitioner of the reason you need their assistance, what you want to achieve and to decide upon a treatment, if applicable.

As you can see there is a need for an exchange of information between you and the healthcare practitioner, so that you both understand the various stages of the decision-making process for you at that particular point in time.

If you don't have all the information you need to be able to reach a decision, you need to tell your healthcare practitioner this, so that they can give you the necessary information. Likewise, if the healthcare practitioner needs further information from you before they are able to suggest a form of treatment or advise about different treatment options, they will ask you for this.

Healthcare decision-making is not always a simple process, and you may need to engage with the process several times and make several treatment decisions. Because of the different roles that you and the healthcare practitioner have in the healthcare decision-making process, it should be thought of as a partnership between you and the healthcare practitioner. Healthcare decision-making is sometimes referred to as shared decision making because of this partnership approach.

Seeing healthcare decision-making as a shared process acknowledges that although the healthcare practitioner is the expert in investigating, diagnosing, or treating healthcare conditions, you are the expert regarding your own body, your healthcare needs and how these affect you. It is also you who knows what you want to achieve.

In shared healthcare decision-making, a further role of the healthcare practitioner is to ensure that you have all the information that you need to be able to make a decision. This does not mean that the healthcare practitioner will just provide you with a lot of information and leave you to make a decision on your own. As well as providing you with the necessary information, they should also support you through the decision-making process. This will include ensuring that you understand your condition and the various treatment options available to you, the various differences between the options, the risks and benefits of each, how they may affect your condition, and what outcomes you could expect from each.

Although a healthcare practitioner may advise you, and support you through the decision-making process, they do not have the right to make a decision on your behalf. The right to make the decision on what treatment you will receive to address your healthcare needs is yours.

Wanting a different treatment to the one being offered to you

As noted above, healthcare practitioners are experts in assessing healthcare needs and offering appropriate treatments to meet those needs. Any treatment that a healthcare practitioner offers to you is one that they consider will address your specific healthcare need(s) and will have a benefit for you. That does not mean that it will be the treatment that you want to receive. It is possible that there are alternative treatments, one of which you would prefer, that are not being offered to you.

While you can ask for a specific treatment to be provided, your healthcare practitioner does not have to offer it if they do not believe that it is clinically appropriate for you. In fact, if they think that it is not clinically appropriate to meet your specific healthcare needs, they cannot offer that treatment to you, because if they did, they would be in breach of their legal duty of care to you.

You are legally entitled to choose between any treatment options that are offered to you by a healthcare practitioner. You are also legally entitled to refuse to accept any treatment that is offered to you by a healthcare practitioner. The decision to accept treatment is yours and yours alone. However, your legal right with regard to choosing a treatment is that you can only choose between the treatments that a healthcare practitioner is willing to offer to you. You can ask for a different treatment, but there is no obligation on a healthcare practitioner to provide it to you.

If you do ask for a specific treatment that your healthcare practitioner does not believe is clinically appropriate for your needs, you should explain the reasoning behind asking for it and why you think it will meet your healthcare needs. If your healthcare practitioner still considers it inappropriate for you, they should explain why and explain why they consider that the treatment they are offering you is appropriate.

There are times when the cost of a specific treatment is relevant. If there are two treatments that will meet your healthcare needs, you may find that you are offered the lower costing one. This is not saying that you are not worth the higher cost of the other one, just that if the lower cost option will meet your needs, it makes economic sense for that to be offered to you first. In some cases, healthcare practitioners may not be able to offer certain treatments because of their cost.

If, after a thorough discussion, you find that you and your healthcare practitioner do not agree on treatment options, you could ask for a second opinion.

Second opinions

There are occasions when you may want to seek a second opinion about the treatment that is being proposed for you. You may even find that your healthcare practitioner suggests that you seek a second opinion if you are unsure about whether to have a particular treatment or if there are considerable consequences of the treatment. On some occasions, your own healthcare practitioner may refer you to another healthcare practitioner so that you can obtain a second opinion about your condition and proposed treatment.

Some patients want a second opinion because they disagree with their diagnosis or the treatment options they have been given. Other patients may want a second opinion because their healthcare practitioner will not provide a specific treatment they are asking for, and they want to ask a different healthcare practitioner if they will provide it.

You do not have a legally enforceable right to demand a second opinion, but it is recognised that patients may request one and this is encouraged. Indeed, the General Medical Council in its code of conduct for doctors has a requirement that all doctors *respect the patient's right to seek a second opinion* (General Medical Council 2020 at page 8). This means that your request for a second opinion should be respected, where possible to do so, unless it is considered not to be in your best interests to request one.

It is possible you won't receive a second opinion because there is no other healthcare practitioner who specialises in the area of medicine that your condition requires within an appropriate distance. Another factor in determining whether you receive a second opinion is that of time. If a delay to you receiving treatment may lead to a worsening of your condition or the chances of a successful outcome, you may find that a second opinion is not considered to be in your best interests and so not provided.

If you want a second opinion, you should raise this with your existing healthcare practitioner and discuss the reasons why you think a second opinion would be of use to you. Depending upon your personal situation, your healthcare practitioner may either refer you for a second opinion or suggest that you contact your GP and ask them to refer you to another healthcare practitioner for a second opinion.

Being referred for a second opinion, whether by your original healthcare practitioner or by your GP, essentially means that you are being seen by a different healthcare practitioner as if it were the first referral, meaning that you may have to undergo the same investigations that you have already had. The second healthcare practitioner should have access to the records made by the first healthcare practitioner.

Once you have the benefit of the second opinion, you could either choose to go back to your original healthcare practitioner and ask them to provide any treatment you need, or you could ask the healthcare practitioner who provided the second opinion to take over your future care and treatment. It is possible that the healthcare practitioner who provides the second opinion will not be able to take over your care and treatment because they do not have the capacity, or they can only accept you as a patient for treatment sometime in the future.

If a second opinion is suggested to you by your healthcare practitioner, they should give you the clear reason why they think this is in your best interests. It may be that your healthcare practitioner wants a more specialised opinion about your condition or because your condition is complicated and requires the input of healthcare practitioners from different specialities.

Choosing a practitioner

The relationship between you and those healthcare practitioners who provide your care and treatment is one that should be based on mutual trust and understanding. Choosing who provides your care and treatment, and where that care and treatment is provided to you, is part of the process in establishing the necessary trust and understanding.

In chapter 1 *Rights*, when discussing healthcare rights, we noted that you can choose which GP or GP practice you apply to be registered with. We also noted that whilst you can ask for your preferred choice, it may not always be possible for this to be provided.

The same situation exists when considering who you would want to provide your care and treatment. If your GP needs to refer you for a specialist opinion or for a specific form of treatment, you have a choice as to what hospital or clinic etc you go to for your specialist appointment or to receive the treatment. You can also request that you see a particular healthcare practitioner. However, in a similar way as when you choose to register with a particular GP or GP practice, in the NHS, your choice of healthcare practitioner or hospital is not a legal right. As such, you can expect to have your preference taken into account but there may be reasons why your preference cannot be accommodated.

Reasons why you may not be treated by your preferred healthcare practitioner, or in your preferred healthcare location include:

- You need to be treated in an emergency; in which case you will usually be taken to the nearest location that deals with that type of emergency.
- You need maternity services, and you will normally be allocated to the nearest location that has availability and can provide the service that you and your baby need.
- The condition you have has a specific waiting time limit for the period from referral to when you are first seen by a specialist, for instance cancer services, and your choice of hospital would not be able to meet that time limit.
- Your preferred healthcare practitioner does not treat the type of condition you have, so you would be referred to a healthcare practitioner who does.

- Your local hospital or other preferred hospital does not provide the service that you need, for instance not all hospitals provide all cancer services. So, you would be referred to a hospital that does provide the service you need.
- You are being referred for a specialist opinion or treatment, and the healthcare practitioner referring you may want a particular specialist to be involved in your care and treatment.

Generally, you can exercise choice in who you will be treated by and where you will be treated until you have had your first appointment with them, after which it is assumed that your treatment will continue to be provided by them at that location. As an example, if your GP needs to refer you to a chest specialist, you could ask to be seen by Dr X at Hospital Y. Once you have had that first appointment with Dr X unless you have an issue with your care or treatment Dr X will be your doctor at Hospital Y for the duration of your treatment.

Requesting a healthcare practitioner of the same sex

In addition to asking for a referral to a particular healthcare practitioner, you are also entitled to make a more general request to be referred to a healthcare practitioner of the same sex as you. You will find that, where possible, a reasonable request will be accommodated. However, you don't have a right to only be seen by a healthcare practitioner of the same sex as you, even if an intimate examination is required. The reason that you don't have a legally enforceable right to only be treated by a healthcare practitioner of the same sex as you is because there is no guarantee that one will be available to treat you at a specific time and place.

If you feel that would like a person of the same sex present during an intimate examination and one is not available to undertake the examination itself, consider asking for a chaperone to be present (see below) if one is not offered to you.

Wanting a different healthcare practitioner

There may be times when you want to have your care and treatment provided by a different healthcare practitioner; not because you want one of the same sex as you or because you want to be referred to a specific healthcare practitioner, but just because you don't get on with your current healthcare practitioner. As noted earlier, healthcare is a partnership between the patient and their healthcare practitioner, and the best partnerships work when there is mutual trust and understanding between the two parties.

If you find that your relationship with your healthcare practitioner is strained or not functioning as you would want, you need to raise this. It can be difficult to raise this with the individual concerned, but ideally this is the best person to raise it with initially. It may be that the healthcare practitioner is unaware that you are dissatisfied, or even that they are behaving in way that they believe you want. If you have an advocate (see chapter 1 *Rights*), they can help you to express this decision.

Discussing it with the healthcare practitioner may alleviate the issue and allow for a working relationship to be established. If, however, you are unable to reach an understanding, you may need to speak to the healthcare practitioner's manager and explain your reasoning for wanting to be treated by another healthcare practitioner.

If your request is reasonable and it is possible to be transferred to the care of another healthcare practitioner, the manager will usually arrange this. However, as with most requests regarding treatment, this is not a legal right, and it may not be possible to transfer your care to a different healthcare practitioner.

It is possible that your current healthcare practitioner is the only practitioner available who specialises in the kind of treatment that you require and transferring your care to another healthcare practitioner would be detrimental to your treatment.

If you are not able to be transferred to the care of another healthcare practitioner, your current healthcare practitioner should remain professional and not treat you any differently because you requested your treatment to be transferred to a different healthcare practitioner. If something has happened that has resulted in you wanting a different practitioner to take over your treatment or care, chapter 8, *Questioning healthcare*, considers what you can do in these situations.

Requesting online appointments

Many healthcare consultations, particularly those that are follow-up appointments, can be conducted by telephone or online.

A request by a patient to have a follow-up appointment via telephone or online will be given due consideration unless there is a compelling reason not to. Such reasons include that an examination will be needed as part of the appointment, or physical treatment will be given. In a similar way, if a patient wants to have a face-to-face appointment when they are only being offered an online or telephone appointment, so long as the patient explains why they believe a face-to-face appointment is required, for instance they need to have a clinical examination, this should be taken into consideration.

Both authors know healthcare practitioners who prefer to have at least some of their patient consultations online because it means that their time is used more efficiently, and they can 'see' more patients than they could in the same amount of time spent having face-to-face consultations.

As with many requests discussed so far, this is something that you may request but cannot legally enforce, so it is a request and not a right as there may be valid therapeutic reasons why it may not be possible.

☽ Relatives, next of kin and carers

We generally all think we know what a relative and a next of kin is. We probably know who our relatives are and who we *want* as our next of kin, but it is questionable whether we know what role either of these have in addressing our healthcare needs. As to carers, this is probably more straightforward but still worth considering.

☽ Relatives

There are two main forms of relatives: those that you have a blood relationship to, and those that you have a legal relationship to.

A blood relative is quite simply those individuals with whom you share common ancestors. You and your relative are said to share a bloodline because you are descended from one person in the past and so are biologically related to them. This could be a father or grandmother or a great grandfather and so on. As examples of blood relatives you may have, you and your blood sister share a parent, you and your blood cousin share a common grandparent. Your birth parent is a blood relative because you originate from them. Blood relatives also include half-blood relationships as well, so a half-sister or half-brother, because there is still blood in common through one of the parents.

The other form of relative you may have come across is referred to as a legal relative because the relationship does not exist because of being a biological relationship, but because of a legal arrangement. A legal arrangement could be an adoption or a marriage or civil partnership. For instance, if your mother were to remarry and her husband has a daughter of his own, that daughter would be your sister. Officially, she would be known as your stepsister to differentiate her from your sister or half-sister, those you have a blood connection to. For many families, this distinction is not acknowledged, and all siblings are either brother or sister without any qualifier.

The usual recognition of a legal relative is those who have 'in-law' in the title. So, a mother-in-law or a brother-in law are both related to you not because you share a common ancestor but because they joined the family as a result of a union between them and one of your blood relatives, or because you have a union with one of their blood relatives. A relative is therefore someone who is connected to you either though a blood line or by an affinity.

⚡ *Next of Kin*

Next of kin is an odd term. We say this because it is a term that we all use and we probably all know what we mean when we use it, but we are probably all using it differently and incorrectly!

There is a common usage of the term next of kin that is taken to mean a person who can speak for the patient, or on behalf of the patient, when the patient is unable to do so themselves. Some people – in fact, many people including some healthcare practitioners – believe that the person who is next of kin has legal rights that allow them to undertake a legally recognised role.

This is not in fact true and there is no legal basis for a next of kin. Being someone's next of kin is not a legal role. There is no official recognition of a next of kin nor who should be a particular patient's next of kin. In fact, a person may nominate anyone as their next of kin.

Lindsay and Marc are both married to other people. It may be expected that we would nominate our respective spouses as our next of kin. But there is nothing to stop us from nominating each other as our next of kin, or indeed anyone else we feel like nominating. (For clarity, we have not nominated one another!)

The only limitation on who you nominate as your next of kin is that the person you nominate has to agree to act as your next of kin. This may have you thinking, so if it is not a formal or legal role, what exactly is a next of kin? Kind of you to ask. A next of kin, when used in a healthcare setting, is just the term used for the person you want to be contacted about your admission to hospital, or other healthcare setting, or to be kept informed about your care and treatment.

Next of kin have no rights to be involved in the patient's care or treatment, other than being given information at the patient's request.

⚸ Carers

Carers UK (n.d.) define a carer as '*a person of any age who provides unpaid care and support to a family member, friend or neighbour who is disabled, has an illness or long-term condition, or who needs extra help as they grow older.*' In this book the term 'carer' is used to describe someone who provides care to a patient but does so in an unpaid capacity and without whom the patient would not be able to manage their daily life. Carers may be family members or a friend or a volunteer from a charity or a patient support organisation. The carer may also be the patient's child. A link to the Carers UK website is included in the resources section.

The key distinction we are making is that a carer is not a healthcare practitioner whose role it is to provide care and treatment to the patient. Rather, the carer does it because the patient needs the care that the carer is giving, and without them the patient would not have their needs met and would not be able to function fully.

The role of a carer can be vital to a patient, yet some carers may not see themselves as carers. They instead may just consider that they are helping their mother or son or brother, as a 'good relative' does, as opposed to having a role outside of the family relationship they have with the patient.

⚥ Nearest relative & qualifying relationships

In some areas of healthcare, you may see the term 'nearest relative' and/or 'qualifying relationship' used.

'Nearest relative' is generally used when talking about relatives and mental health healthcare. This is because mental health legislation, specifically the Mental Health Act 1983, allows relatives to perform specific roles and have defined responsibilities when the patient is subject to the provisions of mental health legislation.

Similar to mental health legislation use of 'nearest relative', organ donation legislation recognises a role for relatives in relation to decisions regarding the donation of a patient's organs after death. The term used in organ donation legislation is 'individuals in a qualifying relationship'.

The 'nearest relative' and their role is discussed in chapter 5 *When the patient lacks the capacity to consent for their own healthcare needs*, while that of 'individuals in a qualifying relationship' is discussed in chapter 7 *Decision-making around the end of life.*

Chaperones

Chaperones are distinct from relatives and carers who may attend an appointment with the patient, and from the advocates discussed in chapter 1 *Rights*. A chaperone is usually a healthcare practitioner who acts as an impartial observer during the time a patient is having an intimate examination. An intimate examination is one where the breasts, genitals or rectum need to be exposed, observed or touched.

The chaperone's role is to ensure that patients are supported during the intimate examination and that the examination is respectful and the patient's dignity is maintained. The chaperone is also present to ensure that the healthcare practitioner undertaking the examination is supported as well, as some patients can cause an intimate examination to be distressful for the healthcare practitioner.

Generally, the chaperone will be someone who is able to undertake the intimate examination or understand the examination, so that they can observe that it was performed correctly. The chaperone should be present throughout the whole of the examination and be positioned so that they are able to observe the healthcare practitioner's actions, as well as be able to provide reassurance to the patient. A chaperone should be the same sex as the patient.

Being offered a chaperone

Healthcare practitioners should offer patients a chaperone before an intimate examination. As well as intimate examinations, a chaperone may also be offered if the patient is one considered to be vulnerable, or a minor who is unaccompanied, and may need reassurance during a non-intimate examination.

Sometimes a chaperone may be offered not because the healthcare practitioner needs to perform an intimate examination, or because the patient is vulnerable, but because the healthcare practitioner needs to invade the patient's personal space. That could be to stand very close to the patient to undertake some other examination such as listening to their breathing, for example.

A chaperone may be offered to the patient even if the healthcare practitioner is the same sex as the patient. If a chaperone is present during a patient's examination this should be recorded in the patient notes.

Refusing a chaperone

There is no obligation for a patient to accept the presence of a chaperone, but a healthcare practitioner may refuse to proceed with an intimate examination unless a chaperone is present. One reason for this is because, rarely, patients have been known to make allegations against healthcare practitioners, and the practitioner may want to protect themselves from such allegations.

If the healthcare practitioner feels that the intimate examination is needed but is not willing to do it themselves without the presence of a chaperone, the healthcare practitioner may refer the patient to a colleague. If a patient refuses to have a chaperone present during an examination, it is to be expected that the healthcare practitioner will record this in the patient's notes.

↗ Relatives as chaperones

A relative should not act as a chaperone as they are not an impartial observer, which is the role of a chaperone. There is nothing that prevents a relative also being present along with a chaperone if both the patient and the healthcare practitioner agree to this.

Requesting a chaperone at an appointment

If a chaperone is not offered to you but you feel that you would like one to be present, whether for an intimate examination or not, you should ask for a chaperone to be provided. If the healthcare practitioner was not expecting to provide a chaperone, you may find that your consultation is delayed while a chaperone is arranged and during this time you may be asked to wait, and the healthcare practitioner may see other patients.

When a chaperone is not available

There may be times when a patient requests a chaperone and it is not possible to provide one, or to provide one of the same sex as the patient. If this happens, the healthcare practitioner will usually offer the patient an alternative appointment when the examination can be undertaken in the presence of a chaperone.

You should not be pressurised into having an examination without the presence of a chaperone when you have requested a chaperone be present. If the timing of an alternative may delay your diagnosis and treatment, you should expect to be told this so that you can make a considered decision. However, it is still your choice as to whether you have the examination without a chaperone or wait until a chaperone is available.

CHAPTER 3

AGREEING TO TREATMENT

The main focus of this chapter is on patient agreement to treatment. There is a brief discussion of what healthcare needs are, alongside treatment choice and treatment decisions, before examining the legal right to treatment. This leads into the main focus of the chapter which is an examination of consent in healthcare. We discuss the need for consent in healthcare before looking at what legally valid consent is, and what is necessary for consent from a patient to be considered legally valid.

The three components of legally valid consent are considered, including a discussion of how competence is assessed and how much information a patient needs to receive for the patient to be judged to be adequately informed.

The difference between assent and consent is explored, as well as terminology related to consent and competence.

The chapter considers the differences between the ability of an adult and a child patient to give their own consent, including a definition of what a child is from a legal perspective. The role of parents in a child's healthcare is examined, including their rights and responsibilities in relation to the child, and a discussion of what parental responsibility is and who may have it in relation to a child. There is consideration of conflicts that can arise between patients and healthcare practitioners when treatment choices are being made, as well as between parents and child patients, and healthcare practitioners and parents. Finally, the ways that a patient can give consent are outlined.

Healthcare and treatment

Healthcare is concerned with meeting a patient's healthcare needs. However, it is not as simple as it may seem from that sentence. Patients may not know what their actual needs are or may believe that they have a need for X, whereas it is actually Y that has to be addressed. For example, a patient may have blurred vision and consider that they have a need that can be met by going to their opticians and having an eye test, and maybe a pair of glasses prescribed for them. However, the optometrist may discover that the patient has the early stages of diabetes and that they need to be seen by a specialist to receive advice and treatment for diabetes.

As we know from chapter 1 *Rights*, you have a right to be registered with a general practitioner (GP) and to have them assess your healthcare needs. Chapter 1 also stated that the GP is the gatekeeper to you assessing the full range of healthcare. It is the GP who will assess what your initial need is, its urgency, and decide which part of the healthcare service you will be referred to.

It is the GP who ensures that patients are seen by the appropriate healthcare practitioner who can fully assess the patient's need and then either provide treatment to meet that need or refer the patient to a healthcare practitioner who is able to.

Because there can be more than one way of meeting an individual patient's healthcare need, there may be treatment options that that patient has to choose between.

Treatment choice

Choice can be both a benefit and a burden. Knowing that there is a choice in the treatment that you are being offered to meet your healthcare needs can mean that you are able to choose the treatment that you are more agreeable to receiving. However, having more than one treatment option offered to you by your healthcare practitioner means that you have to make a choice. If there was only one treatment that is available for your particular healthcare need, your choice is between having it or not. With each option offered to you there is a choice whether to have a specific treatment, a different one, an alternative, or none at all.

Treatment decisions

Knowing which treatment to agree to can be difficult and the role of the healthcare practitioner is to assist the decision-making process and provide information that will help the patient to make their decision. The process of healthcare decision-making is discussed in chapter 2 *Engaging with healthcare*.

Many patients ask their healthcare practitioner for advice when they are offered a treatment option, particularly when there is more than one choice being offered. The role of the healthcare practitioner is to help you meet your healthcare needs, therefore asking them for their advice and their guidance is acceptable as it can be said to be a part of that role. By helping you to make a choice, they are supporting you in choosing an option that is appropriate in meeting your healthcare needs. However, there is a line that healthcare practitioners need to be careful not to cross and which you, as patient, should resist encouraging them to cross. It is not your responsibility as a patient to explain to a healthcare practitioner that they should not be making treatment choices for you.

A healthcare practitioner can advise you when asked. They can tell you which option they would choose. They can even tell you what they would do if they were in your shoes. However, they cannot make the decision for you; that is the line which must not be crossed. The decision about whether to accept treatment at all, and what treatment to choose if there is more than one treatment available to you, is yours.

Conflicts of opinion

Given that there is seldom only one treatment option that will meet your healthcare needs, it is likely that you will have to make a choice between several treatment options. It is also possible that the treatment you choose is not the one that your healthcare practitioner is advising you to have. If this situation were to occur, it needs to be remembered that the purpose of providing healthcare is to meet the healthcare needs of the patient and that the patient has the autonomy to choose the treatment option that they consider is best for them. As noted in the previous section, the role of the healthcare practitioner is to advise you and to assist you in your decision-making, but they cannot make the decision for you or substitute their decision for you if they disagree with your decision.

In chapter 2 *Engaging with healthcare*, when we were discussing the situation if you wanted a different treatment to the one a healthcare practitioner was offering to you, we noted that you only have the right to choose between any treatment options that are offered to you by a healthcare practitioner. A healthcare practitioner can only offer treatment to you if they consider that it will address your specific healthcare need(s) and will have a benefit for you.

This means that if you have decided to accept a specific treatment, the healthcare practitioner must have offered it to you, or another healthcare practitioner did. Either way, you have a right to accept that treatment as it has been offered to you. The healthcare practitioner can put their reasons to you as to why they consider that an alternative treatment is more appropriate for you and to meet your healthcare needs, but they cannot stop you having the treatment that you have been offered and you have accepted.

In the extreme situation where the healthcare practitioner will not provide the treatment to you, they are legally obliged to refer you to another healthcare practitioner who will undertake the treatment for you. The healthcare practitioner still needs to care for and treat you until that other healthcare practitioner is able to take over your care and treatment. A failure to provide you with the necessary care and treatment would be a dereliction of their duty of care to you.

Conflicts of opinion between chid patients and their parents, and also between parents and healthcare practitioners, are considered below when we discuss consent and the child and parental responsibility.

The legal right to treatment

The preceding chapters have noted aspects of patient rights regarding treatment decisions. Some patients may want a particular treatment, or a treatment that is different to the one that being offered to them by their healthcare practitioner.

If there is no right to treatment, then there cannot be a right to demand a particular treatment or to insist that a different treatment is given to you. This is based on the fact that there is no absolute legal right to treatment.

Treatment is offered to you based on an assessment by a healthcare practitioner of your need, and what treatment may meet that need. Your right to treatment is thus conditional on being assessed and there being an appropriate treatment that can be offered to you. The main factor in what treatment is offered to you is the healthcare practitioner and what they consider will meet your healthcare need(s).

As part of the discussion in chapter 2 *Engaging with healthcare*, it was stated that healthcare practitioners can only provide treatment that they consider will be of benefit to you in meeting your healthcare needs. If you want to have a specific treatment and request this from your healthcare practitioner, they can only agree to provide it where it is considered by them to be in your best interests. If they do not believe that the specific treatment you are asking for is clinically appropriate for you, they cannot lawfully provide that treatment to you.

In short, your right regarding treatment options is to be able to choose between the treatment options that are being offered to you by a healthcare practitioner.

Treatment decision-making – a reminder

The key point to be made about healthcare treatment and choosing a treatment is that it is the patient who has the choice. You have the right to choose whether you accept treatment and, where there is a choice, which of the treatment options you will have. It is the legal concept of consent that protects this right.

Consent in healthcare

Consent can be thought of as permission; permission granted by one person for another person to do something. Consent is not unique to healthcare but is a vital aspect of healthcare practice. Without consent, healthcare would not be possible as there would be no legal basis upon which treatment could be provided to patients who are competent to make their own treatment decisions. As will see later in this chapter and in chapter 5 *When the patient lacks the capacity to consent for their own healthcare needs*, different legal principles apply when a patient is assessed as not being competent to be able to give their consent.

The need for consent

Consent is the mechanism whereby the ethical concepts of autonomy and self-determination, as discussed in chapter 2 *Engaging with healthcare*, are given legal recognition and standing. In chapter 2, it was stated that autonomy is the ability of a patient to make their own decisions about their own healthcare needs, even when others disagree with the choices they are making. Without the legal standing of consent, patients would not have the right to be autonomous to make their own healthcare decisions. Because consent is a legal principle, a patient's right to consent is a right that can be enforced in the courts if necessary.

Consent in the healthcare context is an example of how the law works to protect ethical rights and make them enforceable.

As we will see later in this chapter, because of the legal right to consent, not only are the rights of a competent patient to consent to their own treatment protected, but legal mechanisms exist for those patients who do not have the competence to consent on their own behalf. If patients were not able to exercise their right to autonomy and self-determination, that is to make their own healthcare decisions, someone else would have to make treatment decisions for them. As we saw in chapter 2, this is what happens in the paternalistic approach to healthcare. Healthcare practitioners, acting as the expert, make the decision for the patient, who is seen as needing the expert's ability to decide upon the best course of action for them.

It is consent and the acknowledgment that patients have the right to make their own treatment decisions that has enabled the move away from paternalism as the dominant form of healthcare practice that existed in previous decades.

There is another reason why consent is needed in healthcare. This is because it is unlawful to touch another person without their permission, or a lawful reason. Coupled with this is the fact that it is not legally possible, save for some very specific exceptions, for you to give permission to someone to do something that results in your own harm. The exceptions are quite complex and intricate, but in essence you cannot give permission for something that results in an injury unless that injury is a trivial one.

Together, this means that a healthcare practitioner cannot touch you without your permission and you cannot lawfully give permission to them to do something that would result in an injury to you. You would not be able to legally give permission for a healthcare practitioner to cut you, as they need to during an operation, as the cut results in an injury to you and is unlawful.

If a healthcare practitioner were to cut you during an operation, they would be committing a crime. Bear with us on this! A crime has three elements to it. There is the actual act, in our example, the cutting of you. Then there is what was in the mind of the person. Did they intend to cut you and cause an injury? In our example, they did. Finally, there is the absence of a defence. Did the person who cut you have a lawful reason to do so? As you cannot give permission for your own harm, they cannot have a lawful reason, and therefore they have no defence.

Now, this is where healthcare consent comes into play. Consent from a patient is a lawful defence to causing harm to a patient. This means that when a patient has given their consent, the healthcare practitioner can use this as a lawful reason for their action and so will not have committed a crime. Consent is an exception to the legal rule that you cannot give permission for your own harm. The reason for the exception is that the harm you are giving permission for is outweighed by the potential benefit of receiving that harm.

There are therefore two reasons why consent in healthcare is important:

- it enables patients to exercise their autonomy and self-determination
- it acts as a defence for healthcare practitioners against being accused of committing a crime against their patient

Legally valid consent

You have seen in this chapter that consent is the legal way of protecting your right to decide what happens to your body, your self-determination, and your autonomy to make decisions. Because you have a right to make a decision about the care and treatment you receive, and legally this is through your ability to give consent to those treatments you wish to have, there are legal requirements that have to be met before it is acknowledged that you have legally provided your consent and the care and treatment can proceed. Legally valid consent is shorthand for 'consent that has been given by a patient in a way that meets the legal requirements for consent at the time at which the consent was given'. You can see why we have chosen to use the term legally valid consent rather than write that out each time!

Before we see what those legal requirements are, let's look at some terminology related to consent and the giving of permission that you may come across in your healthcare experiences:

- Assent – this is discussed below.
- Consent – you may see consent used to mean any and all of the various processes around the granting of permission by you to a healthcare practitioner in relation to your care and treatment.
- Consent process – this usually refers to the way in which the healthcare practitioner obtains your permission for specific care and treatment to be given to you.
- Informed consent – you may hear your healthcare practitioner telling you that they are asking for your informed consent, or you may see a consent form that you are being asked to sign headed 'informed consent for X' where X is the treatment or procedure they are advising you to have. Informed consent is an American legal term and also an ethical concept. It refers to when a patient

has received all the information that is available, and then is able to make a fully informed choice about a specific treatment. As we will see shortly, there is no requirement in UK law for informed consent.

- Legally valid consent – the term we use and one that simply means that the permission you have given meets the legal consent requirements.
- Patient permission – bit of an odd one this, and not in use much now, but unfortunately still used. It is taken to mean that the patient has given their permission for X to happen but does not go as far as to state that consent has been given by the patient or indeed if that consent was legally valid.
- Valid consent – just a shortened way of saying legally valid consent.

For consent to be acknowledged as being legally valid, it has to meet three requirements. These are that the consent is:

- given by a competent person,
- who is adequately informed,
- and is consenting voluntarily and without being under any form of duress

The first two of these requirements have very specific criteria applied to them and so will be discussed below in greater detail. The third requirement is less complex.

Acting voluntarily

Consent is concerned with a patient exercising their autonomy by making their own decisions about their body and the care and treatment they will receive. The main point about the requirement that consent is voluntary is that it must be a free decision made by a person who believes that they have a choice. If the patient does not believe that they have a free choice, or if the patient is acting under duress to make a particular decision, they will not be acting voluntarily.

Duress could be applied by a healthcare practitioner who believes that a particular treatment is best for the patient and is 'persuading' the patient to accept the treatment. If the 'persuasion' goes beyond that considered acceptable into pressure or undue influence, the patient will be said to be acting under duress. Alternatively, a relative could be the person 'persuading' the patient to accept a certain treatment. If the patient is not making a voluntary decision, then any permission they give to a healthcare practitioner will not be legally valid consent and so the consent could not be relied upon by the healthcare practitioner to justify their actions.

Consent vs assent

Consent is the express giving of permission for some event to happen, from a competent individual, who is acting voluntarily on adequate information about the proposed event.

Assent is not consent. Neither is it permission from an individual. Rather, assent is an agreement that something can happen. So, you are probably thinking, what is the difference between permission for an event to happen and agreement that it can happen? Good question!

Permission is granted when someone is in a position that they can give or withhold permission and decide to grant it. An agreement to go along with something does not mean that the person has the right to withhold their permission, but it does indicate that they agree with the proposed event even if they are not formally able to provide their consent. They want that event to happen.

Some people see assent as meaning that the patient is just not refusing; that they just acquiesce to a particular event. However, this is not the case. Assent is more than the absence of refusal or a simple reluctant acceptance. To assent to some event, the patient has to agree to it happening, even if they are not able to formally consent to it.

There are times when it would not be possible to obtain a legally valid consent. This is usually because the patient lacks the capacity to consent and so, as we saw above, is therefore not able to consent for themselves. This will be discussed further in chapter 5 *When the patient lacks the capacity to consent for their own healthcare needs,* when we consider treatment when a patient lacks the capacity to provide consent for their own healthcare needs. However, even though the patient may not be able to satisfy the legal requirements necessary for consent, they can still indicate whether they wish for a particular aspect of their care or treatment to proceed. Healthcare practitioners can, and should, obtain the patient's assent to care and treatment when the patient is not able to consent but is able to express an opinion.

Consent and the competent adult

When discussing legally valid consent, we stated that one of the requirements is that consent is given by a competent person. In this section we are going to explore what a competent person is.

Terminology around competence

Before we look at what competence is and how it can be assessed, we need to have a slight detour into terminology around competence and when competence is lacking.

Competence and capacity are both used to describe someone who has the ability to make their own decisions about treatment and to give their consent. Some people make a distinction based on the age of the patient, for instance they use the word capacity when the patient is 16 and above and the word competence for those patients under 16.

Others use the word competent when a decision is made by a court as to someone's ability to make decisions, as in 'the court judged that they are competent to make a decision', and use the word capacity when the healthcare practitioner is assessing a patient's ability to make a decision, as in 'the nurse assessed X as having the capacity to make a decision about their treatment options'. To be honest, for our purposes there is not much in it as to which word we should use, but as we are talking about rights that can be enforced, we will go with competence. The issue with this is when the patient lacks competence. What term should we use for that?

The opposite of competent is incompetent but that is quite a loaded term and could be deeply offensive to some individuals, because the use of incompetent suggests in quite a negative way that a person can't do something.

As an example, we both have different abilities with regard to DIY and Lindsay is better at this than Marc. In fact, Lindsay may say that by comparison to her, Marc is relatively incompetent in DIY. Now, that is not to say that Lindsay is being disrespectful to Marc, just that there is a difference in their respective abilities, and Marc can't do something she can. But, if someone was just reading the statement from Lindsay that Marc is incompetent in relation to DIY, they could just take this as a negative comment about Marc, or that Marc is absolutely useless at DIY, or both. However, the situation could be that Lindsay is a brilliant DIYer and should be doing DIY as a side-line, and Marc is average. The point is that the use of the word incompetent has connotations that may not be intended.

It is probably true to say that people engaging with healthcare services and parents and carers would find it an uncomfortable word at least, if not offensive. Would anyone be happy to hear their mum or son called incompetent? Probably not! When lawyers and healthcare practitioners use the word 'incompetent', they are not using it in the everyday language sense but as a way of describing someone who lacks the ability to make a decision.

We won't be using the word incompetent here because of its negative connotations. To describe someone who does not have the ability to make their own treatment decision, we will use phrases based on 'the person who lacks competence' or, 'the person who lacks the capacity to make a decision'.

Competence and consent

Competence in relation to consent in a healthcare context is a two-part ability. Competence means the ability of a person to make a decision, and to be able to communicate that decision to someone else. If the patient is either not able to make a decision or is able to make a decision but is not able to communicate that decision to others, they would not legally be considered to be competent and so would be unable to give their own consent.

Making a decision involves assessing the information that is available and reaching a conclusion as to which course of action, which treatment option, the patient believes is in their best interests or they prefer. Many legal cases have considered the nature of competence and whether individual patients have competence in relation to their own healthcare needs. Prior to the implementation of the Mental Capacity Act 2005, on 1st October 2007, it was only by taking a case to court that a decision could be made on an individual's competence. However, the Mental Capacity Act 2005 now outlines the legal principles which must be applied when determining if a particular patient has competence at a particular point in time.

Having the Mental Capacity Act 2005 in place does not mean that no legal cases are ever brought to determine if a patient has competence or not, as both healthcare and the law evolve and there are situations that occur which were not envisaged in the Act. There can be different healthcare opinions as to a person's competence and these need a final decision to be made. However, in the normal day to day healthcare setting, the provisions in the Mental Capacity Act 2005 make the determination of a patient's competence to make their own treatment decisions less cumbersome.

Assessing competence

It is the Mental Capacity Act 2005 that contains the detail of how an assessment of a person's ability to make their own decisions should be undertaken. The starting point in the Mental Capacity Act 2005 is that every individual over the age of 16 is deemed to be competent to make their own treatment decisions unless it can be proved otherwise.

The presumption of competence is an important one for patients as it means they do not have to prove anything in relation to their competence. It is up to others to prove that the patient lacks the ability to make a decision or to communicate that decision. This is a departure from the time before the implementation of the Mental Capacity Act 2005, when it was the patient who was required to prove their competence if it was ever called into question.

According to section 2 of the Mental Capacity Act 2005, a person cannot be determined to lack the ability to make a decision based solely on their age or appearance or how they are behaving. Before someone can be said to lack the capacity to make their own decision regarding their healthcare needs under the principles in the Mental Capacity Act 2005, two things need to be proved.

The first is that the person has a *'an impairment of, or a disturbance in the functioning of, the mind or brain'* (section 2.1 Mental Capacity Act 2005). The second is that because of this impairment or disturbance, the patient is unable to make a decision or to communicate that decision to others.

Section 3(1) of the Mental Capacity Act 2005 states that a *'person is unable to make a decision for himself if he is unable—*

(a) to understand the information relevant to the decision,
(b) to retain that information,
(c) to use or weigh that information as part of the process of making the decision, or
(d) to communicate his decision (whether by talking, using sign language or any other means)'.

If the patient is unable to do any of a to d, this would mean that they are deemed to lack the ability to make their own decision.

Declaring that someone is unable to make their own decisions has severe consequences for the individual. It means that they lose the right to autonomy and self-determination. However, the Mental Capacity Act 2005 has some further protections in place. These state that a person cannot be said not to understand information unless that information has been given to them in a way that is appropriate to them. This means that the information should be given in their own language or using sign language or any other appropriate means of communication for that particular person. An interpreter may be necessary for some patients before it can be said that they lack the ability to understand the information they are being given.

The person does not have to retain the information given to them indefinitely, they only need to retain it for the purpose of making their decision. A competent patient is able to make any decision they want. The fact that they make a decision that others would regard as unwise or irresponsible does not mean that they are unable to make a decision.

A patient can only be said to be unable to communicate a decision if all reasonable ways to help them have been attempted. If a patient is unable to speak, it would be reasonable to use a communication aid. If the patient requires someone to interpret for them, it would be reasonable for this to be provided before deciding they are unable to communicate their decision.

If a patient has been assessed as not having the competence to make their own healthcare care decision, this should be recorded in the patient's health record along with when, and by whom, the assessment was undertaken.

◘ Who should determine a patient's competence

Firstly, it must be remembered that all patients who have reached the age of 16 are deemed to be competent to make their own decisions unless and until someone assesses that they are not able to do so. The question is, who should be making that assessment?

The healthcare practitioner who is proposing to perform a specific aspect of care or treatment for a patient should be the one who obtains the patient's consent for that care or treatment. Therefore, they should also be the person who assesses the patient's competence if there are any concerns about the patient's ability to make a decision.

However, making an assessment that the patient does not have the competence to make their own decision has such consequences for the patient that not all healthcare practitioners may have the necessary skills. Where this is the case, a relevant specialist healthcare practitioner, who has the appropriate skills, such as a psychiatrist should be consulted or asked to perform the assessment of the patient's competence.

Fluctuating competence

We recognise that so far, we have been discussing competence as if it is an all or nothing situation, and that a patient either has the competence to make their own healthcare decision or they don't. It is not quite as clear cut as this, and patients may have a fluctuating ability to make their own decisions, or even fluctuating levels of competence.

By a fluctuating ability, we mean that a patient may lack the competence to make a particular decision yesterday, but be competent today, and then lose their ability to make a decision again tomorrow. This could be due to an altering level of consciousness or because of the effect of medication on the patient's ability to comprehend or retain information.

In a similar way, a fluctuating level of competence occurs when a patient has the competence to make some decisions but not for others. For instance, a patient's cognitive impairment may mean that they do not have the ability to make a decision about major heart or brain surgery, because they are unable to consider the consequences and the risks of the surgery, but they do have the ability to make a decision of a lower order such as whether to make a blood test. In this way, a patient's competence could be seen to be time specific or treatment specific. Where a patient is assessed as having a fluctuating level of competence, the decision-making should be left until the patient has the necessary competence where it is possible to do so.

When a patient is not competent to make their own decisions

Given that there are legal principles regarding assessing a patient's competence and their ability to make decisions for their own healthcare needs, it will be the case that some patients will be assessed as not being able to make their own decisions. This raises a number of issues and questions with regard to their treatment and how they can lawfully receive treatment without their consent. Some of these issues centre around who can give consent when the patient is unable to do so themselves.

These issues and questions will be considered in chapter 5 *When the patient lacks the capacity to consent for their own healthcare needs,* which discusses patients who lack the capacity to consent for their own healthcare needs.

Being adequately informed

When discussing legally valid consent, the second requirement for consent to be seen as being legally valid was stated as being that the patient is adequately informed. The reason that there is a requirement for information as part of consent is related to the patient being able to understand their healthcare needs and the treatment options being offered to them.

If a patient is not able to understand their own health care needs or the treatment they are being offered, it can affect their ability to engage in the decision-making process and to actually reach a decision.

The fact that there is a requirement that patients are adequately informed before the consent that they may give is considered to be legally valid consent raises the question of how much information the patient needs to receive for it to meet the requirement of being an adequate amount of information. Therefore, this section will concentrate on information giving by healthcare practitioners as part of the consent process.

The law and information giving

There is no legislation that covers the amount of information that a patient has to receive before any consent that they give is considered to be legally valid consent. Nor is there a legal requirement that the healthcare practitioner tells the patient of every last piece of information about the proposed treatment. It needs to be just enough that the patient is considered adequately informed.

Because there is a lack of legislation and the principle regarding information is rather vague and woolly, several cases have been brought before the courts to determine if a specific patient was given the correct and sufficient information they needed to be able give legally valid consent.

Although legal cases deal with a specific set of facts to reach a judgment for an individual, the facts and the judgment in a case can be used in subsequent cases which are concerned with similar issues. In this way, a judgment from an individual legal case can be used to expand a legal principle and move from the specific patient in the case to be applied to all subsequent patients. In our discussion, this would be how much information is considered to be adequate.

There are quite a few legal cases that have sought to clarify what information should be provided by a healthcare practitioner to patients in different clinical situations and for different clinical conditions and treatments. We are going to use three legal cases to show how the judgment from a specific set of circumstances can be applied to all patients, and therefore can be used to outline what the legal requirement is with regard to adequate information giving in healthcare.

The three cases are:

- Chatterton v. Gerson [1981]
- Sidaway v Bethlem Royal Hospital Governors [1985]
- Montgomery v Lanarkshire Health Board [2015]

There are some 30+ years between the first and last of these three cases but it was still necessary for the issue of information to be decided by the courts, which gives an indication of the challenges healthcare practitioners can face when considering how much information to give their patients.

Chatterton v Gerson was concerned with whether a healthcare practitioner, in this case a doctor, has to inform a patient of all the risks with regard to an operation. Dr Gerson did not inform his patient Miss Chatterton of a risk before she gave her consent to the operation. The risk in this case was that following an injection near the spinal cord to act as a pain block, numbness and loss of muscle power could occur. Following the injection, Miss Chatterton did experience numbness of her right leg and impaired mobility.

The court judged that a patient only needs to '*be informed in broad terms of the nature of the procedure which is intended*' (at page 265). This judgment means that healthcare practitioners did not need to inform a patient of all the risks and possible complications and outcomes of a procedure and can withhold certain information if they do not consider it relevant for that particular patient. The court also noted that '*if the information is withheld in bad faith*' (at page 265), the consent given by the patient would not be legally valid.

The judgment in Chatterton v Gerson effectively allowed a healthcare practitioner to decide what information they gave to a patient about a procedure, so long as the patient had a broad understanding of the procedure.

The case of Sidaway v Bethlem Royal Hospital Governors involved a healthcare practitioner who did not warn a patient of a 1% risk of a complication arising. The complication did in fact arise and the court had to decide that if a healthcare practitioner gave the same information as their colleagues, would this be legally acceptable. The court judged that where a healthcare practitioner acted in accordance with accepted practice in relation to providing information to patients, any consent given by a patient would be legally valid.

As a result of the Sidaway v Bethlem Royal Hospital Governors case, a fundamental change to how healthcare practitioners decided on what information they gave to a particular patient occurred. Instead of it being solely at the discretion of individual healthcare practitioners as to what information they gave to their patients, they now had to follow accepted practice as to what information it was appropriate to share with patients.

The Montgomery v Lanarkshire case concerned Mrs Montgomery who was in the later stages of pregnancy and was not warned that if she had a vaginal delivery her baby may be born with severe disabilities. Mrs Montgomery did not have a caesarean section and her baby was subsequently born with severe disabilities. The doctor said that she did not warn Mrs Montgomery of the risks associated with vaginal delivery because they were low, whereas Mrs Montgomery said that if she had been told of the risk, even if was low, she would have had a caesarean delivery.

The court judged that a healthcare practitioner has a duty to *'to ensure that the patient is aware of any material risks involved in any recommended treatment'* and whether something is material is based on whether *'the particular patient would be likely to attach significance to it'* (at paragraph 87)

The result of the Montgomery v Lanarkshire case is that the healthcare practitioner has to determine what the patient considers to be important in meeting their healthcare needs and give information that is appropriate for that individual patient. Information now has to be patient specific in order for any consent given by a patient that is based on that information to be legally valid.

Patient based information

Because of the current legal standard on information giving, as discussed in the previous section, information that is given by a healthcare practitioner should be specific to the patient who is requesting their services. The information must be sufficient to meet the needs of that specific patient. It must allow the patient to understand their condition and the treatment that the healthcare practitioner is proposing they have and to base their decision-making on.

The type of information that a patient who is being advised to have an operation would be told includes:

- what is wrong with them
- what operation is being proposed
- what the operation will achieve in terms of their condition
- the benefits and the risks of the options
- the possible consequences of not having the operation
- any risks and complications
- what the healthcare practitioner proposes if a risk or complication happens
- any alternatives to the operation

A patient can say that they don't want specific pieces of information, for instance possible risk and complications, or that they have enough information. However, if a patient does say this, it is likely that the healthcare practitioner will record the fact that the patient has refused the information. This is so that the patient cannot later claim that they were not told something that is material.

There is no obligation on a patient to receive all the information that a healthcare practitioner wishes to share with them. Being adequately informed is based on individual needs. If the patient believes they have adequate information on which to make a decision, this is likely to meet the legal requirement. The key is that the patient is able to understand what is happening and what treatment is being proposed and can make a decision using the information they do have. In short, that they are adequately informed.

Informed consent vs adequate information

We stated earlier that informed consent is not a legal requirement in the UK for consent to be legally claimed. We will now explain why.

The legal requirement regarding information giving in relation to consent is that the patient has to be adequately informed, and whether a patient is adequately informed is subjective to that patient.

If there was a legal requirement for informed consent, it would be legally compulsory that all patients receive all the information regarding a particular operation or treatment, regardless of whether the patient wanted to receive it all or not. It would reduce the patient's autonomy to decide what information they wanted.

The Montgomery v Lanarkshire case also recognised that there are circumstances when giving a particular patient certain information regarding risks associated with particular treatments could pose a problem for the patient. Additionally, it showed that healthcare practitioners need to be legally '*entitled to withhold from the patient information as to a risk if he reasonably considers that its disclosure would be seriously detrimental to the patient's health*' (at paragraph 88).

There is also the situation where a patient needs to be treated as a matter of urgency and there is not sufficient time to disclose all the relevant information to the patient. A healthcare practitioner may give the most pressing and pertinent information, but not everything that they would share if the need for the treatment was not so urgent. If there was a legal requirement for informed consent, any consent given by the patient in this situation would not be legally valid consent as they would not have been given all the information.

Because of this, the legal requirement is that a patient is adequately informed for their specific needs.

📖 *Withholding information from a patient*

We are going to repeat some points we have made in the preceding section so that it is clear when a healthcare practitioner can withhold information from a patient.

Healthcare practitioners are under a duty to provide all material information to a patient based on that patient's particular needs, so that the patient is adequately informed and able to make a decision.

However, there are two exceptions to this duty:

- when the healthcare practitioner reasonably considers that sharing the information with a patient would be seriously detrimental to the patient's health
- where the patient is unable to make a decision and the treatment is needed urgently.

The way the information is given is important

Patients need to be adequately informed before they are able to give legally valid consent. If a patient cannot understand the information they have been given, they cannot be adequately informed.

Information therefore needs to be given to patients:

- in language that they will understand, not using jargon or terms the patient is unfamiliar with
- in their own language, or using an interpreter if the healthcare practitioner and patient do not share a language
- through non-verbal means such as printed literature if appropriate for the patient.

Consent and the child patient

In this section we will look at the ways in which a child can give their own consent to treatment.

Definition of a child

There are various legal definitions that relate to the under 18s.

The Children and Young Persons Act 1933 in section 107 defines a child as someone under 14 and a young person as someone over 14 but under 18.

A child is legally defined in the Children Act 1989, section 108, as someone under the age of 18. This is also the definition adopted in Article 1 of the United Nations Convention on the Rights of the Child.

You may sometimes see a person under the age of 18 referred to as a minor. This refers to the fact that they have not reached the legal age of majority. The Family Law Reform Act 1969 reduced the age of majority from 21 to 18.

Another term used in relation to individuals under the age of 18 is young person. This is generally used to refer to someone who has reached the age of 16 but is under 18. When young person is used, a child is then said to be someone under the age of 16.

We are going to use the legal definition in the Children Act 1989 that anyone under the age of 18 is called a child.

Giving consent as a child

The first point to note is that, as with an adult, only a competent child can legally give consent on their own behalf. This means that we need to consider at what point a child is legally competent.

This is relatively straightforward for those child patients aged 16 and over because, as noted earlier when examining how competence is assessed, the Mental Capacity Act 2005 states that every individual over the age of 16 is deemed to be competent to make their own treatment decisions unless it can be proved otherwise. Section 8 of the Family Law Reform Act

1969 also gives a child aged 16 or over the right to consent on their own behalf.

The issue arises for those patients who are under 16. This is because the presumption of competence that applies to every patient aged 16 or over, where they are deemed to be competent unless it can be proved that they lack the competence to consent, does not apply to patients under the age of 16.

There is no legislation which gives a patient under the age of 16 the right to consent on their own behalf for their healthcare needs. To determine the rights that a child under 16 has, we have to turn to case law.

The legal right of a child under 16 to give their own consent is contained in the case of Gillick v. West Norfolk and Wisbech Area Health Authority and another [1985]. This case was brought by a mother (Mrs Gillick) in response to guidance issued to general practitioners (GPs) by the Department of Health and Social Security that a GP who gave advice or prescribed contraceptives to a girl under 16 would not be acting unlawfully. Mrs Gillick did not want her daughters who were under 16 to receive contraceptive advice or treatment without her knowledge or consent.

Effectively, Mrs Gillick was asking the court to confirm that the consent of a parent should be necessary before healthcare advice or treatment could lawfully be given to a child under 16, which was the legal position at the time of the case.

Rather than upholding the legal position of the time, the court stated that a child under 16 was able to give consent on their own behalf when they could demonstrate that they had the sufficient intellectual and emotional maturity to understand fully the decision they were being asked to make.

This was a very important case in regard to the rights of a child. As a consequence of the case, rather than there being a position that no child under 16 was able to consent for themselves at any time, a child who is able to demonstrate their competence can provide their own consent.

Because a child patient aged under 16 has to prove that they are competent to consent on their own behalf, and this principle was established in the Gillick case, the principle is referred to as Gillick competence. A child who can demonstrate that they are competent to make their own healthcare decisions is said to be 'Gillick competent'.

Whether or not a child is deemed to be Gillick competent is an assessment that has to be made by the healthcare practitioner who is proposing to treat the child. The assessment of the child's competence needs to be made for each and every treatment decision, at the time the decision is needed.

The assessment as to whether a particular patient under 16 has the necessary competence is based on whether they have the sufficient maturity to be able to comprehend the decision they are being asked to make and understand its gravity and relevance. This means that the child will need to be able to demonstrate that they understand their condition, what treatment is needed and why, the potential benefits of the treatment along with any possible complications or side effects, and the consequences of both having the treatment and not having it.

Due to the rigorous requirements to be able to prove that they are in fact Gillick competent for a specific healthcare decision, not all children under 16 will be able to successfully meet the requirements. It is possible to think of Gillick competence as a scale where the older the child is, the more likely it is that they will meet the requirements.

In a similar way, as with adult patients who may be assessed as competent for some decisions but not others, so a child may be assessed as being Gillick competent for healthcare decisions that have less serious consequences for them but not for other healthcare decisions which have more serious consequences. As the child's emotional and intellectual development progresses, so does their ability to be assessed as having Gillick competence.

If a child patient changes their mind frequently about a

particular healthcare decision, this could be taken as evidence that they lack the maturity sufficient to make that decision, and so they are not actually Gillick competent in relation to that decision.

Hopefully it can be seen that a patient under the age of 16 is in an entirely different legal position regarding being able to make their own treatment decisions. This is because once a child reaches the age of 16, rather than have to rely upon being assessed as being Gillick competent they have protection in legislation which automatically presumes they are competent and so provides them with the legal right to give their own consent.

Parental responsibility & rights

Parental responsibility was briefly mentioned in chapter 1, *Rights,* when we discussed advocacy and the child. Here, we will take the opportunity to examine parental responsibility.

We are going to use the word 'parent' to mean someone with parental responsibility. This is just shorthand and should be taken to mean anyone who has parental responsibility for that particular child.

⚡ Rights and responsibilities

Parental responsibility is probably best defined using the definition in the Children Act 1989, where section 3(1) states that *'parental responsibility means all the rights, duties, powers, responsibilities and authority which by law a parent of a child has in relation to the child and his property'.*

Parental responsibility exists until the child reaches the age of 18. As stated in the definition, it gives the parent certain rights and responsibilities in relation to the child for whom they have that parental responsibility.

These rights and responsibilities include:

- The right to name the child
- The right to have the child brought up in a particular religion
- The right to participate in the child's education, with a responsibility to ensure that the child attends some form of education
- The right to information about their child's healthcare and their needs and treatment, and the right to make healthcare decisions for the child with a responsibility to ensure that the child has their healthcare needs met

The parent's rights exist to allow them to exercise their responsibility for the child, acknowledging that the child's needs are paramount, not the parent's. Any action a parent takes as a result of their parental responsibility for a child has to be taken to achieve what is best for the child and not might be best or more convenient for the parent.

Those who have parental responsibility

Because of the importance that is attached to parental responsibility due to the implications it can have for the child over which the parental responsibility can be exercised, a quite complex set of laws have emerged as to who has parental responsibility. Although we could probably devote a whole chapter to go through all the various laws and their intricacies, given that we are just looking at parental responsibility from a healthcare perspective, we are going to make some general points regarding who has parental responsibility.

Birth mothers have parental responsibility, even if they are acting under a surrogacy arrangement.

Fathers have parental responsibility if they are married to the mother at the time the child is born. If they are not married to the mother, they can also have parental responsibility through a parental responsibility agreement with the mother, or through a court order. A father will also have parental responsibility for a child if they are named on the child's birth certificate. This last point only applies to children born since specific dates; these are since:

- 15th April 2002 in Northern Ireland
- 1st December 2003 in England and Wales
- 4th May 2006 in Scotland

Female civil partners or spouses of the birth mother have parental responsibility if the child was conceived by assisted reproduction.

A second female parent can acquire parental responsibility where the child was not conceived via assisted reproduction if they are registered as a parent of the child, or if the birth mother enters into a formal agreement with them, or through a court order.

Stepparents can acquire parental responsibility if they marry or enter into a civil partnership with someone who has parental responsibility for the child and have the agreement of all individuals with parental responsibility. Any disagreement can be considered by the courts.

Adoptive parents will normally have parental responsibility transferred to them from the natural parents as part of the adoption process.

Local Authorities may have parental responsibility for children in their care, through an emergency protection order, a care order, or other court order. This is generally shared with the parents unless the parent's parental responsibility has been removed from them through a court order.

If the parents place a child in care voluntarily, then they would normally retain sole parental responsibility.

A legally appointed guardian, or someone who is caring

for a child under a residency order, may have sole parental responsibility or share it with the parents.

Fosters parents do not have full parental responsibility for the children they look after. This will remain with the parents and/or the Local Authority. However, they do have a form of limited parental responsibility in that they are generally able to make decisions about the child relating to their day-by-day care and needs. The decisions they are able to make are usually agreed beforehand with their social worker and the child's social worker. More significant or longer-term decisions remain with those who have full parental responsibility.

Parental responsibility cannot be given up, but it is possible to arrange for someone to temporarily step in and exercise the rights and duties of someone with parental responsibility with the permission of the person who actually has parental responsibility for the child. This is usually in situations where a grandparent or a carer may be temporarily looking after the child, or a teacher.

Getting divorced does not remove the parental responsibility either parent has.

Parental responsibility can only be removed from someone by a court order.

☙ When parents disagree about their child's treatment

Parents are individuals and may have different opinions as to what is in their child's best interests, and so reach a different answer when asked to give their consent for a particular treatment that the healthcare practitioner wants to provide for their child. Legally this is not a problem, as consent is only needed from one person with parental responsibility. Therefore, so long as one parent considers that it is in their child's best interests to receive a particular treatment and is willing to give their consent, the healthcare practitioner is legally entitled to act on that consent.

If parents disagree you may find that the healthcare practitioners will not go ahead with a procedure but will instead try to gain consent from both parents before proceeding. If it is not possible to get the parents to agree on a course of treatment it is possible to go to court and have the court make a declaration as to the lawfulness of the proposed treatment. This is generally only used in life-threatening situations.

There are exceptions to the fact that consent is only needed from one parent with parental responsibility. This is where the proposed procedure is non-therapeutic. That is, it is not being given to meet a healthcare need. This would include procedures such as a non-therapeutic circumcision and immunisations that are not routinely administered to children.

✒ When healthcare practitioners don't agree with parents

In the healthcare context, if a healthcare practitioner believes that a parent is not making care and treatment decisions in the best interests of the child, they can challenge this in the courts, and ask the court to give a judgment on what care and treatment the child should receive.

Obviously, a healthcare practitioner should not try and make an application for a court hearing just because they disagree with a decision the parent is making on behalf of their child. The healthcare practitioner is best advised to consider why they believe the parent is not acting in the child's best interests, prior to raising the issue with a more senior member of staff.

Some factors to consider when a parent may be thought to be acting contrary to the child's best interests:

- is the parent making decisions that a reasonable parent would make?
- the relationship between the parent and the child

- is the child disagreeing with the decision that the parent is making?
- the extent of the treatment. Is it invasive or does it have severe or serious consequences for the child's future?

A parent's competence to make decisions under their parental responsibility can be questioned in the same way that a patient's can. There is the same presumption that a person over 16 has the competence to make their own decisions, even if that decision is being made under parental responsibility for someone else. However, if there is a reason to believe a parent does not have the competence to make a particular decision for their child, the option to have the parent assessed exists.

The only reason that a healthcare practitioner can challenge a parent's decision is if a parent is not acting in their child's best interests. A healthcare practitioner is not able to insist that a parent agree to a particular treatment just because they believe the child needs it. This would be an act of paternalism. It is the parent who is held to know what is best for their child, and the healthcare practitioner's role to advise the parent, not to make the decision themselves.

A healthcare practitioner cannot therefore overrule the decision that a parent makes in their child's best interests. If a parent is in the situation where they and the healthcare practitioner disagree on the treatment for the child, for instance if the healthcare practitioner wants the child to have a treatment that the parent doesn't want them to have, the parent needs to explain that they do not want the child to have the treatment. If this does not relieve the situation, they should ask to see the healthcare practitioner's manager and explain the situation or ask to see another healthcare practitioner regarding their child's healthcare needs. Either way, the parent does not have to accept treatment that they do not believe is in their child's best interests.

Ways of giving consent

There are three main ways in which consent may be given or obtained. These are:

- Written
- Orally
- Implied/inferred

There is no legal requirement that consent is provided by the patient in a written format. Consent that is given orally is as legally valid as consent which has been given by the patient via a signature on a consent form that is subsequently kept in the patient's notes.

So long as the three principles outlined above are met, that is consent is given voluntarily by a competent patient, who is adequately informed, that consent will be valid regardless of the method by which it has been given.

Written consent

It is more common to see written consent being requested by healthcare practitioners when the treatment in question is more invasive or the outcome has more severe consequence for the patient. Thus, surgical operations will usually require written consent from a patient whereas undergoing a chest x-ray will not usually require written consent.

You may find that some healthcare organisations require healthcare practitioners to have a written record of consent before a certain treatment is provided. They may even have standard consent forms for certain procedures and treatments, for example a standard consent form for an appendectomy and another standard form that is used for heart surgery.

Where a standard consent form is used, you will most likely find that the healthcare practitioner will adapt the form for your specific circumstances. This may mean that certain parts of the form are crossed through as they do not relate to your treatment or that the healthcare practitioner adds to the form so that the specifics of your individual circumstances are included. These alterations and additions should be undertaken by the healthcare practitioner prior to you signing the form.

The reason that healthcare practitioners adapt standard consent forms to your specific needs and circumstances is because your healthcare needs and your treatment is unique to you. Whilst the healthcare practitioner may have seen your condition and your treatment many, many times, the treatment is tailored for you and to meet your healthcare needs. Although there is some commonality in what you and others need, and the treatment they have received is similar to what you will receive, a standard consent form allows the form to be specific to you and your circumstances, whilst also ensuring that all the common points are covered and pre-printed.

There is also one other point that really needs to be made about consent forms. This is that the fact there is a signed consent form does not in itself mean that legally valid consent has been given by the patient for a specific treatment. The presence of the consent form indicates that the patient, at some point in time, was asked to sign the form and did so. It also suggests that there has been a discussion between the healthcare practitioner and the patient, but not the extent of that discussion. Legally valid consent is only present when the principles above are fulfilled. This will be the case whether a consent form is signed or not, and just having a consent form signed does not mean that the patient has given legally valid consent on its own. There may be other reasons why the consent form was signed, such as undue pressure or the healthcare practitioner being paternalistic.

The signed consent form can also be used if a patient claims that they never gave their consent to a particular treatment, and it was therefore performed unlawfully. The fact that a consent form has been signed does not mean that consent has been given by a patient, and they can be refuted, but it is a good indication that a discussion was held between a patient and healthcare practitioner and to refute it the patient would need to explain why they signed the form if it was not to indicate their consent.

Oral consent

You may find that your healthcare practitioner asks you if you are happy to proceed with a particular investigation or treatment. This is their way of obtaining your oral consent. If you say yes, you are giving your consent. There is nothing wrong with this approach to obtaining consent, and it is the most common method of obtaining consent from a patient.

Of course, you will expect us to make a little caveat here. We won't disappoint you. The caveat is that the patient who is being asked if they are happy to proceed with the specified investigation or treatment has to be competent, be acting voluntarily and be adequately informed about the investigation or treatment. Provided these three criteria are met, oral consent is as legally valid as written consent.

Now if Marc, acting as a nurse, was to approach Lindsay and ask her if she knew she was scheduled to have an operation today and Lindsay replied yes, this would be highly unlikely to be seen as legally valid consent because:

- although Lindsay is competent until proved otherwise
- she may not understand what the operation entails, what it is for or what the outcome and consequences may be
- she has not actually given any permission, but merely stated that she is aware that her operation is scheduled for today.

When a patient has provided their consent orally, the health-care practitioner will usually make a record of this in the patient's health records. This may note the date and time that the consent was given, any specific information that was given to the patient and/or any questions that the patient asked, and the responses given. If there was another healthcare practitioner who acted as a witness to the patient providing their consent, their name may be recorded, and they may also sign the health record as well.

Implied consent and inferred consent

The terms 'implied consent' and 'inferred consent' are used a lot in healthcare. However, they are often used in an inappropriate way and neither in fact refers to legally valid consent.

Implied consent refers to a situation where the actions of a patient are said to imply that the patient wants something to happen. Inferred consent is when a healthcare practitioner infers from the patient's action that they want the thing to happen. So, both implied consent and inferred consent can relate to the same action by the patient but from different perspectives.

An example may help. Suppose a healthcare practitioner approaches you as you are sitting in a ward and tells you that they need to take a sample of blood from you. In response, you roll up the sleeve of your coat and the healthcare practitioner takes a sample of blood from you. It is said that your action of rolling up your sleeve implies that you are giving your consent for the blood to be taken. The healthcare practitioner would use the fact that you rolled up your sleeve to say that they infer from your action that you are giving them consent to take your blood.

The reason that implied consent and inferred consent do not indicate legally valid consent is that for consent to be legally valid, it has to be given voluntarily by a competent patient who has been adequately informed. At no point in the above example are you given any further information. You are not asked for permission for the blood to be taken, and neither do you expressly give your consent for the blood to be taken.

Rather than giving your consent, you may be under the impression that you have no choice but to have your blood taken and so are not acting voluntarily but because you 'have' to have your blood taken. In this case, there can be no legally valid consent because you, the patient, is acting involuntarily. Rather, the patient can be said to be not objecting rather than giving their consent.

When it is used, implied consent or inferred consent is generally only used for routine care and treatment. At one time it was probably the most common way in which 'consent' was obtained in the healthcare environment. Indeed, some people believe(d) that if a patient was in hospital, they are agreeing to be treated and no further consent is needed as their action of being present in hospital implies that further treatment has their consent. In fact, each and every aspect of care or treatment needs its own consent to be obtained. Turning up for an outpatient appointment does not mean that you are giving a blanket consent for any treatment that the healthcare practitioner believes you need to meet the healthcare need you attended the department for.

Nowadays, most healthcare practitioners would not assume that patients have given their consent simply because they are present in a clinical area, but instead would ensure that they have actual express consent from a patient before undertaking any form of care or treatment for a patient.

⏰ Turning inferred consent into legally valid consent

As noted above, using inferred consent is not actual consent from a patient. Yet, it is relatively straightforward to turn the example used earlier of taking a patient's blood into a legally valid consent. The main thing that needs to be done to move on from inferred consent is to not tell the patient that you need to do something, but to ask them a question which requires them to give you permission to do that thing.

So, instead of approaching a patient who is sitting in a ward and telling them that you need to take a sample of blood from them, approach the patient and explain that you have been asked to take a sample of blood to be tested and ask if it is OK that you do that. If the patient says yes, you have oral consent, legally valid oral consent, rather than relying upon your interpretation of the patient's action.

Time for consent

There is no set limit on the amount of time you have in which to make a treatment decision. A healthcare practitioner should give you as much time as you need to be able to weigh up all the information you have and then to make a decision based on your needs and wants.

The only limitation on taking as much time as you need is the urgency with which any treatment needs to be given to you. It may be the situation that if you do not have treatment X within a certain timeframe, which can be hours not days, it will not be possible to proceed with treatment X and you will have to have treatment Y instead. Therefore, the more urgent it is that you receive the treatment, the less time you may have to make a decision.

CHAPTER 4

REFUSING TREATMENT

So far, we have discussed consent in this book in the positive, as a way of you giving permission for specific care and treatment offered to you by a healthcare practitioner. This chapter starts by recapping what consent is before considering whether consent is a single event or one that lasts continually after it has been given. Chapter 4 then moves on to examine the situation if you decide you don't want a specific treatment: the other side of the 'right to consent'. This includes a discussion of your right not to accept treatment that is offered to you, whether as an adult or a child patient, including self-discharge.

The chapter also looks at how a patient can change their mind about a treatment by looking at when a patient can withdraw their consent for a specific treatment.

Finally, chapter 4 considers the situation of healthcare practitioners who do not want to provide certain treatments and what their legal position is, through a consideration of conscientious objection.

A brief recap on consent

We are just going to reiterate the main points about consent in healthcare to facilitate our discussion on how and when patients may be able to refuse to provide their consent for specific treatments. For a fuller discussion of consent in healthcare please see chapter 3 *Agreeing to treatment*.

Consent is a legally recognised right and allows patients to exercise their right to be autonomous and determine what happens to their own bodies. It is unlawful to touch someone without their consent, or another lawful reason.

When a patient gives their consent to a healthcare practitioner it is permission from the patient for the healthcare practitioner to do something, that is, to provide some treatment to them.

For consent to be legally valid, it has to be voluntarily given by a competent person who is adequately informed about their condition and the proposed treatment.

Only competent individuals are allowed to give their consent. Anyone over the age of 16 is automatically assumed to be competent, but a child under 16 has to prove that they are competent. A child under 16 who has proved that they are competent to provide their own consent is known as being Gillick competent.

If there are concerns about a patient's competence and their ability to participate in the decision-making process about their healthcare needs, an assessment can be made of their competence. It is the Mental Capacity Act 2005 that contains the law on competence to consent, including the assumption of competence for those 16 and over, and assessing a patient's competence.

When the patient is a child, someone with parental responsibility can provide consent on the child's behalf.

Consent as a single event or continuous permission

As we have just seen in the recap on consent, consent is needed in healthcare to permit healthcare practitioners to lawfully treat their patients. However, there is often confusion amongst patients and healthcare practitioners as to what the giving of consent by a patient is actually permitting the healthcare practitioner to do.

When a patient gives their consent, what they are effectively saying is that they understand what their healthcare need is, what the healthcare practitioner is proposing to meet that need, and that they have the information they need to make a decision. The permission from the patient to the healthcare practitioner, through the giving of consent, is for the specific treatment.

If a healthcare practitioner wanted to change the treatment, they would need consent from the patient for that change of treatment. It has to be acknowledged, however, that healthcare practitioners may ask the patient to give their consent for alternative treatments at the same time as they give their consent for a primary treatment. This is often used for surgical operations, where the surgeon may not be able to determine the exact procedure that is needed until they have started the operation and after the patient has received their anaesthetic. Having consent from the patient for alternative procedures is safer for the patient, as it may mean the patient does not have to have the operation cancelled and then have another anaesthetic and operation, with the complications this can entail, after the revised procedure has been explained to them and they have given their consent for it. It is likely also that there would be a delay between the original operation and the revised operation.

Consent is generally held to exist from the time it has been given for the specified procedure or treatment until that procedure or treatment has been completed. If the treatment consists of more than one single event, for instance if a patient was receiving treatment for tennis elbow and this necessitated three injections of steroid over a period of time, consent would be sought from the patient for the course of treatments.

At the point at which a healthcare practitioner is going to undertake a treatment with their patient, they need to ensure that a legally valid consent has been obtained from the patient. Most times it will be the healthcare practitioner who is intending to perform the care or treatment who will seek consent from the patient, usually just before the care or treatment is to be provided. However, for more invasive treatments, such as surgical operations, the patient may be asked to give their consent some time in advance of the treatment and at a 'consent clinic' where the patient will be encouraged to ask questions and they can be answered appropriately, although not necessarily by the healthcare practitioner who will perform the treatment.

Where someone other than the healthcare practitioner who is going to perform the treatment received the consent from the patient, the healthcare practitioner who is going to perform the treatment should check that the patient has given their consent, preferably by asking the patient.

What all this means is that just because you may have given your consent for a particular treatment, it is not a 'once and forever' permission. Just because you have given consent now, today, for a treatment to go ahead, does not mean that you are giving your consent in perpetuity. The fact that you have given your consent needs to be checked each and every time you have a treatment, even if you originally gave your consent for a course of treatments.

In a similar way, just because you have attended a hospital, or even been admitted to a hospital ward, does not mean that you have given your consent for anything other than your attendance, or your admission. If the healthcare practitioners caring for you are recommending that you receive further treatment, then they need to obtain your consent for each of those treatments before they can lawfully provide them to you.

Refusal of treatment

If chapter 3 *Agreeing to treatment* is about the legal principles of consent and how consent may be given by a patient, then this chapter, *Refusing treatment*, can be thought of as the opposite side of the consent coin. Together, chapters 3 and 4 provide the full picture of consent and the competent patient.

Throughout this section, we are discussing adult patients who have the competence to make a decision regarding their own healthcare needs and the treatment needed to meet those needs. Child patients and refusal of treatment is discussed in a later section within this chapter.

The question that this section is answering is, 'can a competent patient refuse to have a treatment that is being recommend to them by a healthcare practitioner to meet their healthcare needs'?

The answer to that question should come as no surprise, but let's logically go through the process of answering it so that we can see the ethical and legal basis for the answer.

Points to consider in determining if a patient can refuse to have a treatment:

- It is not lawful to touch someone unless you have their consent or another lawful reason to do so.
- Consent is the legal equivalent of the ethical principle of self-determination, and both are a way of ensuring that patients can exercise their autonomy
- If a healthcare practitioner asks a patient for their consent to a treatment, they are asking for permission to give that treatment to the patient.
- One of the legal principles that needs satisfying for consent to be legally valid is that it is given voluntarily by the patient.

Taken together, these points indicate that if it is legally necessary for a healthcare practitioner to ask for a patient's consent before they can give a particular treatment to the patient, and a patient has a right to determine what happens to their own body, the patient must have the right to give their consent for the treatment or to refuse to give their consent. Otherwise, the giving of consent by a patient is not a voluntary act as the treatment would be given regardless of the patient's response.

Legally, this is correct. If a patient, who has competence to make a decision, refuses to give their consent for a particular treatment, that treatment cannot lawfully be given to that patient. In short, no consent = no treatment.

There are two main ways that a patient could refuse treatment: refusal of one treatment being offered to them in favour of another treatment that may or may not be being offered to them or refusing all treatment. The legal basis for a patient's right to refuse treatment has been questioned in numerous legal cases over the years. There are two cases in particular that clearly state the current legal position.

In 1992, the legal case of Re T had to consider if the patient, Ms T, had given their consent voluntarily. The case was concerned with whether a 20-year-old female had freely refused a blood transfusion or was coerced into doing so by her mother, a practising Jehovah's Witness. As part of the judgment in the case, Lord Donaldson made the declaration that

'*an adult patient who...suffers from no mental incapacity has an absolute right to choose whether to consent to medical treatment, to refuse it or to choose one rather than another of the treatments being offered. ... This right of choice is not limited to decisions which others might regard as sensible. It exists notwithstanding that the reasons for making the choice are rational, irrational, unknown or even non-existent*' (Re T [1992] at page 652–3).

This is quite a clear statement about a patient's right to refuse treatment.

As a result of the judgment in Re T, a patient is legally entitled to refuse to give their consent for any reason they like, or even to refuse to give their consent and not give a reason why they are refusing. It does not matter what others think of the patient's decision. If a healthcare practitioner disagrees with the patient's decision to refuse treatment, or believes that the patient is making an unwise or irrational decision, contrary to the patient's healthcare needs, the patient's refusal is still legally valid.

The only provisos are that the patient is competent to make a decision regarding the treatment they are refusing, the patient is acting voluntarily, and that the patient has been adequately informed about their decision. These three stipulations are discussed further in the next section.

In 2002, the case of Re B extended the legal principle of a patient's right to refuse treatment. The case concerned Ms B, a 43-year-old woman who needed artificial ventilation to maintain her life. Ms B wanted to have the artificial ventilation removed, but knowing that this would cause Ms B's death, the healthcare practitioners caring for her refused to do this. The case was held to determine if it was lawful to remove the artificial ventilation from Ms B.

In the case it was held that Ms B had been unlawfully treated since the point she had stated she wanted the artificial ventilation removed and that 'the right of a competent patient to request the cessation of treatment had to prevail over the natural desire of the medical and nursing profession to try to keep her alive' (Re B [2002] at page 450).

The result of this case is that a competent adult patient can refuse to consent to treatment for any reason whatsoever, even if that refusal will mean that the patient suffers harm, and even if the patient would die as a result of not having the treatment.

The law of healthcare consent means that an adult patient judged as being competent has an absolute choice over whether to accept the treatments they are being offered, and indeed whether to receive any treatment at all. The patient does not have to engage with healthcare practitioners if they do not want to. For instance, a patient does not have to let a healthcare practitioner into their home if they do not want to receive their advice or any treatment. A patient considered to have capacity does not have to have their healthcare needs met if they choose not to.

Legally valid refusal of treatment

A patient has the legal right to refuse treatment, but they have to fulfil the same criteria to refuse treatment as they do to give their consent to accept treatment. The patient has to be competent, adequately informed and acting voluntarily.

Competence to refuse treatment

Only a competent patient is able to refuse treatment. The crucial time is at the point that treatment is to be given. If a patient lacked the competence to give their consent when it was being requested but regained their competence prior to the treatment being given and subsequently refused the treatment, their refusal, subject to the other criteria discussed in this section being met, would be legally valid because a competent adult cannot have treatment given to them against their wishes.

Consider if the situation were reversed, and the patient was competent when the treatment was discussed and they gave their consent, but later when the treatment was to be given, they lacked the competence to make a decision. The treatment could lawfully proceed on the basis that the patient's last competent decision was to have the treatment. As we will discuss in chapter 5 *When the patient lacks the capacity to consent for their own healthcare needs*, there are other lawful ways in which the treatment could be given too.

If there is any doubt about the patient's competence to make a decision to refuse treatment, this can be assessed in the same way as discussed in chapter 3 *Agreeing to treatment*. The principle in the Mental Capacity Act 2005, that every individual over the age of 16 is deemed to be competent to make their own treatment decisions remains, even where the patient is deciding to refuse treatment.

If a competent adult patient refuses to accept treatment, no-one can override that decision and force the treatment onto the patient or substitute their decision for the patients, except in very limited circumstances which are discussed in chapter 5 *When the patient lacks the capacity to consent for their own healthcare needs*. The situation regarding child patients is discussed below.

Having adequate information to refuse treatment

Patients may be intending to refuse to give their consent for a particular treatment, or indeed all treatment, for any number of reasons. For example, this could be because of their personal beliefs, because they do not believe that the treatment will be of benefit to them, or because they fear the treatment or any consequences and complications and what this might mean for them.

As well as being adequately informed to be able to make a decision to accept treatment, there is a requirement that a patient understand the implications of the decision they are making to refuse treatment. There is no minimum level of understanding that a patient needs to have; they just need to have adequate information for their own needs.

If a patient were to refuse treatment that a healthcare practitioner believes is in the patient's best interests to receive, the healthcare practitioner is required to explain to the patient why it is in their best interests to receive it. This would include explaining the reason that the treatment is being offered and what it is expected to achieve regarding meeting the patient's healthcare needs, as well as the consequences for the patient of not receiving that treatment.

If the patient does not believe that the treatment has a benefit for them, the healthcare practitioner should explain their reasoning for recommending it, and what they expect the outcome to be. If the patient's reason for refusing the treatment is fear of the treatment, the healthcare practitioner should listen to the patient and ask them to explain their fears and discuss these with the patient, giving the patient relevant information about the treatment and its possible outcomes and complications.

Although the patient is required to have the information to assist them with their decision-making, what they do with that information is up to them.

Voluntary treatment refusal

When discussing legally valid consent in chapter 3 *Agreeing to treatment*, it was noted that if a patient does not believe that they have a free choice, or if the patient is acting under duress to make a particular decision, they will not be acting voluntarily. Although this was stated in relation to giving consent, it is equally true if a patient wants to refuse to accept a particular treatment or indeed all treatment.

A patient can be placed under duress to refuse a particular treatment or to refuse any and all treatment. This duress could be from a healthcare practitioner who does not believe that a particular treatment is right for the patient, or from a relative.

Withdrawal of consent for treatment

Withdrawal of consent could be seen as being similar to refusing treatment. However, it is different in that consent has already been given by the patient for the treatment, and the patient has subsequently decided that they do not want the treatment and wish to withdraw their consent.

Just because consent has been given by a patient does not

mean that it lasts forever. Consent from a patient for a particular treatment will last until that treatment has been completed, until the treatment is no longer necessary, or until the patient decides that they no longer want to have the treatment.

Withdrawal of consent for a particular treatment can be likened to a patient changing their mind, and a competent patient is legally entitled to change their mind. This is the case even if the withdrawal of their consent will cause harm to the patient. The patient may change their mind for any of the reasons noted above that detail why a patient may refuse to consent in the first place.

At the point at which a patient withdraws their consent, it is as if the consent had never existed. Therefore, if a healthcare practitioner attempted to give a patient a treatment after consent had been withdrawn by a competent patient, they would be acting unethically, unlawfully, and against their professional duty to the patient.

Once notified by the patient that they no longer wish to proceed with the treatment, the healthcare practitioner should stop the treatment. However, the treatment may only be stopped when it is safe to do so. It may not be possible to stop immediately, for instance in the middle of a surgical procedure, and the healthcare practitioner has to ensure the patient's safety. For a surgical procedure, this may mean using stitches to close the wound site.

When a child patient wants to refuse treatment

We are again going to be using the term 'parent' for someone who has parental responsibility for a child.

Parental responsibility and the rights of a parent with regard to their child has been discussed in chapter 3 *Agreeing to treatment*. In that chapter, it was noted that a parent has the right to information about their child's healthcare and their needs and treatment, and the right to make healthcare decisions for the child with a responsibility to ensure that the child has their healthcare needs met. In this section, we will examine parental responsibility in relation to the child patient who wishes to refuse treatment.

We also saw in chapter 3 that a child over 16 or one who has been assessed as being Gillick competent has the right to consent for their own healthcare needs, as an adult patient can.

Section 8(1) of the Family Law Reform Act 1969 states:

'the consent of a minor who has attained the age of sixteen years to any surgical, medical or dental treatment which, in the absence of consent, would constitute a trespass to his person, shall be as effective as it would be if he were of full age; and where a minor has by virtue of this section given an effective consent to any treatment it shall not be necessary to obtain any consent for it from his parent or guardian'.

Because of this a parent cannot overrule a competent child's consent to treatment.

Although section 8 of the Family Law Reform Act 1969 gives children aged 16 and above the right to consent on their own behalf, and a child assessed as being Gillick competent can also consent on their own behalf, neither the Family Law Reform Act 1969 nor the judgment in the Gillick case make any mention of the right of a child to refuse treatment. In addition, the judgment in Re T [1992], which gives an adult patient the right to refuse treatment, explicitly states that it relates to adult patients.

A child patient can simply refuse treatment by not giving their consent. The problem with this is that someone with parental responsibility can exercise their right to make a decision regarding the child's healthcare needs and give consent on behalf of the child. This means that whilst a parent cannot overrule a competent child's consent to treatment, they can overrule their refusal of treatment.

Since only one consent is needed for a treatment to be lawfully given to a patient, and for a child patient this can come from the child or anyone who holds parental responsibility for the child, it is possible to have a situation where the child has refused, one parent has refused and because the other parent has given their consent, a legally valid consent exists which permits a healthcare practitioner to lawfully go ahead with the treatment.

Because consent has been given does not mean that a healthcare practitioner has to give the treatment. They are legally entitled to, but do not have to. The healthcare practitioner may consider that it is not in a child's best interests to force them to have a treatment that they do not want and have refused themselves. The healthcare practitioner has to balance the need for the treatment against the possible psychological and emotional distress that giving the treatment may cause to the child.

Healthcare practitioners working with children try to involve the child in the decision-making process as far as the child is able, even if the child is not able to give consent themselves or where the child has refused to give their consent and the consent for treatment has come from a parent. The aim is to have the child assent to treatment where they cannot consent, and to get a consensus agreement when there is disagreement between the child and their parents.

🕮 *When parents want to refuse treatment for their child*

When the child is under 16 and is not considered to have Gillick competence to give consent for their own healthcare needs, the decision as to whether the child has treatment is the right of the parents. If the parents are not willing to give their consent for treatment to go ahead, the healthcare practitioner is not allowed to lawfully proceed with the treatment.

Parents are expected to act in the best interests of their child.

This is true whether the child is under 16 or aged 16 or 17. As was noted in chapter 3 *Agreeing to treatment*, if a healthcare practitioner does not consider that the parent(s) is acting in the child's best interests, they can challenge the parent's decision, including if the decision was to refuse to have the recommended treatment.

A decision that the healthcare practitioner does not agree with is not the same as the parents acting contrary to the child's best interests. So long as the decision is taken in the child's best interests, a parent may refuse treatment that is offered to meet the child's healthcare needs and may lawfully remove the child from the clinical area, including if this results in the parent discharging the child against the advice of a healthcare practitioner.

An example of a patient refusing to give their consent for treatment that is advised by a healthcare practitioner would be when a parent refuses to give their consent to a blood transfusion because the child is being brought up following the faith of the Jehovah's Witnesses. It could be argued that refusing to allow a child to have a blood transfusion goes against the child's best interests. However, it can also be argued that going against a doctrine of the child's faith is not in the child's best interests. Therefore, any decision for a child is a balancing act of the child's best interests in meeting their healthcare needs against any other competing best interests.

Other ways of going against the advice of a healthcare practitioner

Refusal of treatment, or withdrawing consent once it has been given, can be seen as a patient going against the advice of a healthcare practitioner. Other ways that a patient may go against the advice of a healthcare practitioner include (but are not limited to):

- temporarily leaving a clinical area that the patient has been admitted to
- discharging themselves against the advice of a healthcare practitioner_

Temporarily leaving a clinical area that you have been admitted to

There are many reasons why a patient may want to temporarily leave a clinical area such as a ward. Sometimes, healthcare practitioners may give a patient permission to leave the clinical area for a set period of time. At other times, they may inform the patient that they are not allowed to leave the clinical area, and if they do so and any issues arise these will be the responsibility of the patient. This is because the patient, if they leave the clinical area, will be doing so against the advice of the healthcare practitioners.

The healthcare practitioners in a given clinical area will have responsibility for, and a duty of care to, the patients within that clinical area. Part of this responsibility and duty is to ensure that patients are kept safe. If a patient is outside of the clinical area, the healthcare practitioners cannot observe the patient or provide care and treatment to them. They would therefore be unable to react if the patient's condition deteriorated.

If the patient is competent, the healthcare practitioners cannot legally prevent them from leaving the clinical area.

Discharge oneself against the advice of a healthcare practitioner

Other than when a patient is being held under one of the sections of the Mental Health Act 1983, if a patient wishes to permanently leave a clinical area, they can request to be discharged. If the healthcare practitioners do not consider that it is in the patient's best interests to be discharged at that point, the patient may make the decision to discharge themselves. Patients discharging themselves from hospital and other clinical areas is generally known as self-discharge or discharge against medical advice.

Whilst a healthcare practitioner cannot forcibly prevent a patient from taking their own discharge, they can ask the patient to explain their reason for wanting to leave to determine if there is anything that can be done to persuade the patient to stay. The patient does not have to give their reason.

The healthcare practitioner is under a duty to ensure that the patient is aware of the consequences of their leaving the clinical area. If the patient wishing to self-discharge is you, you may find that the healthcare practitioner working in the clinical area asks you to stay until a more senior healthcare practitioner is available to talk to you about leaving the clinical area. You do not have to stay until someone is available to talk to you, but it may be worth hearing what they have to say and their opinion of the consequences leaving could have for you.

Many clinical areas will have a policy that will result in the healthcare practitioner asking you to sign a form acknowledging that you are aware of the risks you are taking in self-discharging yourself. However, there is no obligation upon you to sign a form acknowledging that you are taking your own discharge from the clinical area.

If you are taking medication whilst in the clinical area as part of your treatment, you may not be given medication to take home if you are self-discharging yourself. It will depend upon whether the healthcare practitioners consider it safe for you to take the medication yourself.

A competent adult patient has the right to take their own discharge even if this is against the advice of their healthcare practitioner(s). If a competent adult patient is prevented by a healthcare practitioner from leaving the clinical area, this could constitute a criminal offence.

Where a patient is not considered to be competent to make the decision to leave the clinical area, whether that be because of their condition or any medication they are taking, the patient will need to be assessed by a healthcare practitioner to determine if they do have the capacity to make the decision to leave or not. If not, then they may be able to be detained in their best interests.

For those patients under 18, someone with parental responsibility can give their consent for the patient to be detained on the clinical area.

If a patient does take their own discharge from a clinical area against the advice of their healthcare practitioner(s), they can expect that this fact is recorded in their healthcare record along with any advice they were given regarding the risks they were taking and any discussion that took place. If the patient signed a form acknowledging the risks they were taking, this will also be kept in the patient's healthcare record.

If the patient is assessed as not having the competence to make the decision to take their own discharge, this will be noted in their health record together with what actions were needed to ensure that the patient stayed in the clinical area.

Conscientious objection

It may seem rather an odd topic to be discussing in a chapter that is concerned with refusing treatment. However, it could be argued that conscientious objection can be seen as a form of refusing treatment. With conscientious objection, rather than the patient being the one who is refusing to be treated, it is the healthcare practitioner who is doing the refusing; in this case refusing to carry out the treatment they object to.

Conscientious objection, when used by healthcare practitioners, also shares another similarity with the rights of a patient. This is that conscientious objection can be said to be a mechanism for healthcare practitioners to exert their autonomy to practise according to their conscience and beliefs.

Healthcare practitioners are expected to provide healthcare to their patients to meet the patient's need according to their skills and abilities. Thus, the only reason for a healthcare practitioner not to provide a specific treatment is because they lack the skills or ability to provide that treatment. Conscientious objection is an exception to this expectation.

A healthcare practitioner who exerts their right to conscientious objection is stating that they have an ethical, moral, or religious objection to a specific treatment and that they do not want to participate in the provision of that treatment because of their beliefs.

Treatments that a healthcare practitioner can lawfully conscientiously object to

The right of a healthcare practitioner to conscientiously object to specific treatments arises in legislation. Over the years, there have been attempts to expand the range to treatments that individual healthcare practitioners may exercise their right to conscientious objection and refuse to participate in.

The last attempt to extend the range of treatments that could be subject to conscientious objection was in 2018. This was through the introduction of the Conscientious Objection (Medical Activities) Bill to the House of Lords. The aim of the Bill was to add the withdrawal of life-sustaining treatment as a treatment that a healthcare practitioner was able to conscientiously object to, and hence not participate in.

The Bill was not passed, and so the withdrawal of life-sustaining treatment is not a treatment that a healthcare practitioner is able to conscientiously object to.

Currently, there are only two areas of treatment that a healthcare practitioner may conscientiously object to. These are:

- Termination of pregnancy
- Activities which are regulated under the Human Fertilisation and Embryology Act 1990

The right not to participate in the termination of pregnancy because of a conscientious objection arises in the Abortion Act 1967 for healthcare practitioners working in England, Scotland or Wales and The Abortion (Northern Ireland) Regulations 2020 for those healthcare practitioners working in Northern Ireland.

The wording in the Abortion Act 1967 states that *'no person shall be under any duty, whether by contract or by any statutory or other legal requirement, to participate in any treatment authorised by this Act to which he has a conscientious objection'* (section 4(1)).

The Human Fertilisation and Embryology Act 1990 regulates assisted conception and embryo research amongst other areas. The right to conscientiously object to participate in these activities is in section 38(1) of the Act which states: *'No person who has a conscientious objection to participating in any activity governed by this Act shall be under any duty, however arising, to do so'*. The Act also states that *'the burden of proof of conscientious objection shall rest on the person claiming to rely on it'* (section 38(2)).

📖 Utilising conscientious objection

If, as a healthcare practitioner, you wish to exert your right to conscientiously object to a treatment and not participate in that specific treatment, you need to be able to demonstrate that you do in fact have an ethical, moral or religious objection to the treatment. Not wanting to participate in providing a certain treatment to a patient is very different to having a conscientious objection to it.

Conscientious objection does not mean providing no treatment

If a healthcare practitioner exercises their right to conscientiously object to participating in the termination of pregnancy or with assisted reproduction, this does not mean that the healthcare practitioner can simply walk away from their patient and does not have to provide any care at all.

The healthcare practitioner who exercises their right to conscientious objection still has a legal duty of care to their patient. The duty of care is superior to the healthcare practitioner's right to conscientious objection and means that the healthcare practitioner can only refuse to particate in treatment where it is safe for them to do so. Practically, this means that healthcare practitioners are required to refer a patient who requires a treatment that they conscientiously object to participate in to another healthcare practitioner. The referring healthcare practitioner legally has to care for and treat their patient until the healthcare practitioner to whom the patient has been referred to can take over the patient's care and treatment.

Another factor in a healthcare practitioner exercising their right to conscientious objection is what aspect of treatment the legislation states can be objected to. As an example, the conscientious objection clause, as it is known, in the Abortion Act 1967 only relates to the actual termination of pregnancy. A healthcare practitioner is still expected to participate in all other areas of the care and treatment of a patient who is undergoing a termination of pregnancy, both before and after the actual termination of pregnancy itself.

CHAPTER 5

WHEN THE PATIENT LACKS THE CAPACITY TO CONSENT FOR THEIR OWN HEALTHCARE NEEDS

In this chapter, we consider situations where a patient is not able to make their own decisions about their treatment options. This can be in emergency situations, or because the patient does not have the ability to make their own decisions due to an illness.

It asks who can make a decision for a patient when the patient can't do so for themselves, and can a healthcare practitioner lawfully provide treatment to patients who lack the capacity to give their consent for that treatment?

The chapter begins by considering the reasons why a patient may lack the capacity to make their own treatment decisions, before examining the way in which treatment may lawfully be given to patients who lack capacity. This includes child and adult patients.

In relation to adult patients, this includes a discussion of advance decisions and lasting power of attorney. For both adult and child patients, it includes a discussion of the principle of necessity and best interests.

Following this is a consideration of how patients may have their liberty restricted, including through mental health legislation, which includes a discussion of the role of relatives, and also through the Deprivation of Liberty Safeguards.

Reasons why a patient may lack the capacity to make their own healthcare decisions

In chapter 3 *Agreeing to treatment*, it was noted that Section 3(1) of the Mental Capacity Act 2005 states that a *'person is unable to make a decision for himself if he is unable—*

>   *(a) to understand the information relevant to the decision,*
>   *(b) to retain that information,*
>   *(c) to use or weigh that information as part of the process of making the decision, or*
>   *(d) to communicate his decision (whether by talking, using sign language or any other means)'.*

Therefore, if a patient is unable to do any of a to d above, they would be said to lack the capacity to make their own healthcare decisions. This would mean that they could not lawfully give their consent for a specific treatment, or indeed to refuse a particular treatment.

There are various reasons why a patient may lack the capacity to make their own healthcare decision and not be able to give a legally valid consent to any treatment option for their healthcare needs. The following are some broad examples to illustrate the reasons why patients may lack the capacity to make treatment decisions:

- If the patient is a child under 16 and they have not been assessed by a healthcare practitioner as having Gillick competence, then legally they lack the competence to make their own healthcare decisions.
- When a patient is unconscious, they would be unable to communicate a decision, even if they could hear what was being said to them.
- Patients who are taking certain medication, such as sedatives and analgesics, may have altered levels of

consciousness and so be unable to make decisions until the effects of the medication have worn off.

- As the Mental Capacity Act 2005 itself states, if a patient has *an impairment of, or a disturbance in the functioning of, the mind or brain'* (section 2.1), this can affect their ability to make a decision regarding their own healthcare needs.
- The effect of physical conditions can affect the patient's cognitive ability. For instance, when the patient's blood glucose level is very low, as can happen with patients who have diabetes. Patients who have lost a lot of blood, for example during a traumatic injury, can have reduced oxygen levels and this may affect their cognitive ability or their level of consciousness.

The actual reason that the patient lacks capacity to make their own treatment decisions is not as important as the fact that, apart from those patients under the age of 16, a patient has to be *assessed* as lacking capacity before they can be said to lack the capacity to give their consent in relation to their own healthcare needs. This is because the Mental Capacity Act 2005 assumes that someone is competent to make their own treatment decisions unless it can be proved they lack the capacity to do so.

The rest of this chapter is based on the assumption that the patient has been assessed as lacking the capacity to make their own treatment decision, unless specifically stated otherwise.

Ways in which treatment can be given when the patient lacks capacity

The ways in which a healthcare practitioner may lawfully treat a patient who lacks the capacity to make their own treatment decisions can only be used with patients who are either under 16 or have been assessed as lacking the capacity to give legally valid consent. This means that a healthcare practitioner would first need to have assisted the patient to make a treatment decision using all reasonable ways possible, as required by section 3 of the Mental Capacity Act 2005. It is only if the assistance provide by the healthcare practitioner does not result in the patient being assessed as having the capacity to make their own decision that the patient will be said to lack capacity.

Patients who have fluctuating levels of capacity

Where patients are assessed as having fluctuating levels of capacity to engage in the decision-making process regarding their own healthcare needs, chapter 3 *Agreeing to treatment* noted that any decision that needs to be made by the patient should be left to a time that the patient's capacity allows them to make that decision. It would only be when it is not possible to leave the making of a decision to a later time that the healthcare practitioner may utilise one of the ways in this section as a lawful reason to provide treatment to the patient.

Lawful ways to treat a patient who lacks capacity to make their own decisions

The following list outlines the ways in which a healthcare practitioner may lawfully provide treatment to a patient when the patient lacks the capacity to be able to make a decision about the treatment themselves.

The list is divided into those patients who are under 18, and those who are 18 or older. This is because once a person reaches the age of 18 in the United Kingdom, no-one can give consent on their behalf, not even a court of law, apart from in some limited exceptions which will be discussed later.

Each of the methods identified in the following list will be discussed further in the sections that follow:

- Patients aged under 18
  - Parental responsibility
  - Inherent jurisdiction of the High Court
  - Principle of necessity
- Patients aged 18 or older
  - Advance decisions
  - Lasting power of attorney
  - Principle of necessity

The child who lacks capacity to consent for themselves

Unlike the ability of a child to give their own consent to treatments, where there is a difference to how those aged 16 and over are considered compared to those under 16, there is no difference to how a child patient is treated when they lack the capacity to provide their own consent to treatment. The discussion that follows is applicable to child patients of any age.

A child patient lacks the capacity to consent for themselves if they are:

- aged 16 or over and have been assessed as lacking capacity,
- under 16 and have not been assessed as being Gillick competent.

The role of parents and others who may hold parental responsibility for a child have been discussed in chapter 3 *Agreeing to treatment*, and chapter 4 *Refusing treatment*. It is not intended to repeat what was discussed in those chapters, save to say that someone with parental responsibility may give consent for treatment to be provided to a patient under the age of 18, and this includes where the child lacks the capacity to engage with the decision-making process.

The sovereign, through its courts, has a duty and authority under what is termed *parens patriae* (meaning parent of the nation or parent of the country) to protect those who cannot protect themselves. It is usually referred to as the inherent jurisdiction of the courts and is limitless in what can be authorised under it. Only the High Court can exercise the power of parens patriae, usually by the judges of the Family Division of the High Court. When the High Court exercises its power under its inherent jurisdiction, it is usually though an Order of the High Court.

Under its inherent jurisdiction, the High Court can provide consent for a child regarding treatment that is needed to address a healthcare need of the child. The High Court can authorise treatment where the child does not have the capacity to give their own consent and it is not possible to obtain consent from someone with parental responsibility. However, the High Court can authorise treatment even if the child and those with parental responsibility will not consent, or are actively refusing the treatment, where the court considers that it is in the child's best interests to receive the treatment.

The principle of necessity applies in the same way to patients of all ages and so will be discussed further when we look at how it is used to lawfully provide treatment to adult patients who lack the capacity to make their own treatment decisions.

Drawing together what we have discussed in chapter 3 *Agreeing to treatment*, chapter 4 *Refusing treatment*, and this chapter, the following two lists show how consent can be provided, or refused, for a child with regard to their healthcare needs:

Treatment can be authorised for a child to meet their healthcare needs by:

- a child under 16 who has been assessed as being Gillick competent
- a child over 16, as they are assumed to be competent
- someone exercising parental responsibility for the child
- an Order of the High Court under its inherent jurisdiction
- using the principle of necessity in an emergency situation.

Treatment can be refused for a child by:

- the child themselves, if they are assessed as being Gillick competent or over 16 AND those with parental responsibility for the child do not overrule their decision.
- someone with parental responsibility

Similar lists for an adult can be found at the end of the *Best interests* section below.

Advance decisions

An advance decision is one of those 'it does what it says on the tin' terms. It is a decision made by a patient in advance of an event happening. There are several different ways that an advance decision can be made by a patient, with different terminology used for these different ways and also for different versions of the same thing.

Terminology in use for advance decisions:

- Advance decision
- Advance directive
- Advance refusal
- Advance statement
- Living will

Advance decision, advance directive, advance refusal, and living will all essentially refer to the same thing. Advance decision is the term used in the Mental Capacity Act 2005, whilst an advanced directive was the term used prior to the Mental Capacity Act 2005 and is a term that arises from common law. Both refer to the situation where a patient makes a declaration when they are competent about treatment they do not want to have if certain conditions are met. Because advance decisions are concerned with treatment the patient does not wish to have, they are sometimes known as advance refusals. 'Living will' is a more common term for the ability of a patient to refuse specific treatment at a later point in time.

An example of an advance decision would be if Marc decided that he would not want to receive artificial ventilation if there was no prospect that he would ever be able to live without the artificial ventilation.

An advance statement is different to the other forms of advance decision, whatever terms is used for them. Advance statements are a declaration of treatment that the patient *does* want at a time when they lack the capacity to make a decision for themselves.

Although an advance statement may seem to be the same as an advance decision or advance directive, there is a major distinction in addition to the fact that the former is requesting some treatment and the latter ones refusing treatment. This distinction relates to the fact that a patient cannot demand a treatment. A patient may only agree to receive treatment that is being offered to them by a healthcare practitioner or to choose between any alternative treatments being offered to them. Allied to this is recognition that a healthcare practitioner is only legally able to give treatment that they believe is clinically necessary. Taken together this means that, whilst a patient is able to refuse any treatment at all, even if the refusal may result in the patient's harm or death, as discussed in chapter 4 *Refusing treatment*, a patient cannot demand any treatment they like and so there is no legal recognition of an advance statement as there is for advance decisions etc.

We will consider advance statements further when we discuss best interests. For now, we are going to continue to discuss advance decisions. The term advance decision is being used for any decision made by the patient that they intend to be used to include advance directive, advance refusal, and living will, and to mean when a patient makes a declaration of treatment that they do not want if certain conditions arise at a later time when they have lost the capacity to make a decision at the time it is needed.

Advance decisions in practice

A patient has to have reached the age of 18 before they are able to make an advance decision, so they do not apply to child patients. Advance decisions can only be made by the person to whom they apply. They cannot be made by a carer for the person to whom they provide care or by a relative or next of kin.

To be valid, an advance decision must be made by a competent patient. There is no requirement that someone makes an advance decision, but if a patient wants to have one, they need to do so before they lose the capacity to make decisions about their healthcare needs.

There is no set manner in which they must be made, and they can be in writing or made orally. If they are written, it makes sense for them to be witnessed. If they are made orally, this has to be communicated to the healthcare practitioners caring for and treating the patient. Having a note in the patient's health records would help to ensure that the relevant healthcare practitioners are aware that an advance decision exists. It is possible to ask a healthcare practitioner to make a note of an oral declaration by a patient.

If a patient wants to refuse life-sustaining treatment, they have to explicitly state that they want to refuse the treatment even if doing so will mean that their life is at risk, or it will result in their death. Also, this is the one time when the advance decision does have to be in writing. It must also be signed by the patient, and it must be witnessed.

There are no requirements regarding the terms that are used, and the patient can use any terms that mean something to them. For instance, artificial ventilation could be written as life support machinery, or just life support.

What does need to be included in an advance decision for it to fulfil what the patient wants is for it to include the treatment that is being refused and the situation or conditions when the patient would not want that treatment. As an example, Lindsay may decide that if she becomes unable to write, she would not want any treatment that would prolong her life including life support or artificial nutrition (that may be a bit extreme, but it helps illustrate the point!)

Advance decisions can only be used when the patient loses their capacity to make their own health care decisions. Until that time, it has no legal validity. Therefore, if a patient finds that they are in a situation where they need treatment that they have previously stated that do they not want in an advance decision, even if the situation they are in is an emergency, provided they have currently got the capacity to make decisions regarding their healthcare, their current decision supersedes the one they made in the advance decision.

A patient can withdraw an advance decision at any time when they have the capacity to do so. If a patient changes their mind about what is in an advance decision, they can make a new one and have the old one destroyed or, if it was made orally, have the note about it in their health record removed and replaced with the new one.

If there is doubt about a patient's advance decision or even about whether a patient actually has an advance decision in force, healthcare practitioners can apply to the courts for a declaration about the lawfulness of any proposed treatment. Whilst they are waiting for the declaration to be made, they can treat the patient in their best interests.

ᛉ Lasting Power of Attorney

Lasting Power of Attorney were introduced by, and are governed by, the Mental Capacity Act 2005. There are two types of Lasting

Power of Attorney (LPA). These are for property and financial affairs, or for health and welfare. It is permissible to have both, and many people do, but we are concerned here with the LPA for health and welfare.

An LPA is the exception we referred to earlier when we were discussing *Lawful ways to treat a patient who lacks capacity to make their own decisions* in chapter 5, and we said that once a person reaches the age of 18 in the United Kingdom, no-one is able to give consent on their behalf, not even a court of law, apart from in some limited exceptions.

This is because an LPA is an authority from one person (known as the donor) to another person (known as the attorney) that allows the attorney to make decisions on behalf of the donor. When an LPA is in effect, the attorney makes decisions on behalf of the donor as if they were the donor.

Unlike advance decisions, because of the wide scope of the authority that can be given from donor to attorney, LPAs can only be completed on a set form, although the form can be completed online or on a paper version. There are certain criteria that must be completed for the LPA to be legally valid:

- The form has to be signed, by
  - The donor
  - Attorney(s)
  - Two witnesses
  - The 'certificate provider', a person who is not the intended donor, attorney or a witness, who confirms that the donor understands what they are signing and is doing so voluntarily.
- The LPA has to be registered with the Office of the Public Guardian, which currently costs £82 per LPA
- If the donor wants the attorney to be able to make decisions regarding life-sustaining treatment, this needs to be specifically stated on the LPA, and there is a section for this on the form.

There is a government website which takes you through the steps of completing and registering an LPA. When completing the LPA, the donor can state how they would like the attorney to act in specific circumstances. An LPA can only be used by the attorney when the donor does not have the capacity to make the decision themselves. Any decision made by an attorney under an LPA has the same effect legally as if it were made by the donor.

If a patient has an advance decision and an LPA, the LPA renders the advance decision redundant. This is because the effect of an LPA is that a healthcare practitioner would seek consent from an attorney for treatment they want to provide to the patient (donor). It is the attorney's consent or refusal of consent which has legal authority.

Attorneys must act in the best interests of the donor. If there is any doubt as to whether the attorney is acting in the donor's best interests, a healthcare practitioner can apply to the courts for a declaration about the lawfulness of the attorney's decision(s). Whilst they are waiting for the declaration to be made, they can treat the patient in their best interests.

If they have the capacity to do so, a donor can request the Office of the Public Guardian to remove an attorney from their LPA. If they want to have another attorney, the donor will need to end their existing LPA and make a new LPA. LPAs can be ended by the donor at any time that they have the capacity to do so. The donor would need to notify the Office of the Public Guardian of the fact that they want the LPA to end. They do not have to have a replacement LPA.

An individual has to have reached the age of 18 before they are able to make an LPA, so they cannot be made by child patients and do not apply to them.

If an attorney gives consent for a treatment to be given to an unconscious, or otherwise incapacitated patient, and later the patient regains consciousness and disagrees with the treatment that was given, there is no cause for complaint against the healthcare practitioner who provided the treatment. This is because the healthcare practitioner will have been acting under a legally valid consent, from the attorney, when they gave the treatment.

Any complaint the patient has will be with the attorney, which is why it is recommended that patients have a discussion with the person they want to appoint as their attorney before the LPA is completed, so that the attorney fully understands the patient's wishes and what they want to happen in given circumstances.

Principle of necessity

There will be adult patients who have neither an advance decision nor an LPA and are considered to lack the capacity to make their own treatment decisions. As we know, no-one can consent for an adult patient without an LPA, not even the courts. This leaves us with a conundrum; a patient has healthcare needs, and a healthcare practitioner cannot meet these needs without the patient's consent or another lawful reason to treat them.

Thankfully, the common law has provided a lawful reason in the principle of necessity. The principle of necessity was explained in the case of F v West Berkshire Health Authority [1989]. F was a 36-year-old female who was unable make decisions for herself due to a mental disorder and was in a sexual relationship. The evidence of those treating her was that she would be psychiatrically harmed if she became pregnant and that sterilisation was necessary in her best interests. F's mother supported this view. In the case, it was stated that where treatment is necessary 'to preserve the life, health or well-being' of a patient (per Lord Goff F v West Berkshire Health Authority [1989] at page 565), and it is not possible to obtain consent, the healthcare practitioner has legal authority to act in the best interests of the patient.

When acting under the principle of necessity, a healthcare practitioner has to:

- act in the patient's best interests,
- do the minimum necessary,
- not go beyond what is immediately needed.

It is the principle of necessity that allows healthcare practitioners to act in emergencies, when the patient lacks capacity and the healthcare practitioners do not know anything about the patient other than their healthcare needs.

If the patient is in need of emergency care and treatment and does not have the capacity to make their own decision, there is no reason to wait to provide treatment, so that someone with parental responsibility can make a decision for a child, or someone acting as an attorney can be consulted under an LPA. The principle of necessity can be used in these situations as the delay would not be in the patient's best interests. The principle of necessity is also known as the doctrine of necessity.

Several times in this book, this chapter, and even in this section, we have referred to treating patients in their best interests, so now we turn to consider what 'best interests' actually refers to.

Best interests

The term *best interests* is a form of shorthand to mean 'what decision on treatment would be best for this particular patient'. It is an objective test and is not meant to merely be the healthcare practitioner making a subjective judgement based on what they would want in a similar situation, nor what they think the patient may want because of the patient's condition or what other patients with similar conditions have decided.

Determining a patient's best interests does not ask what the person would decide if they had the necessary capacity to do so. Rather it seeks to ask, after considering all the information about the patient, what is best for this patient in this set of circumstances. To make it an objective test, a balance must be applied to all the relevant information that is known about the patient. No single piece of information has more importance than another, unless it is known that the patient places a higher emphasis on it than they do other factors. Therefore, what may be in the best interests of one patient may be different to what may be undertaken in the best interests of another patient who is in exactly the same clinical condition, because of the information that is known about each patient.

Best interests as a means of making a decision on what treatment to provide to patients who are unable to make a decision themselves has a basis in both common law and legislation.

Two legal cases, (F v West Berkshire Health Authority [1989] and Re MB [1997]), have stated that treatment can be in a patient's best interests if *'it is carried out in order to either save their lives, or to ensure improvement or prevent deterioration in their physical or mental health'* (F v West Berkshire Health Authority [1989] at page 551). It is important to note that in Re MB, it was noted that the treatment does not have to be medical in nature and can be social treatment or psychological treatment or anything else that provides a benefit to the patient. It can also include treatment that goes beyond their immediate needs, if it is clinically appropriate to have that treatment now rather than wait until it becomes an immediate need.

The Mental Capacity Act 2005 does not state what best interests is but provides guidance as to what needs to be considered to determine what a particular patient's best interests may be. Section 4 states that (note that in the Act 'he' refers to a healthcare practitioner):

5. WHEN A PATIENT LACKS THE CAPACITY

1) *In determining for the purposes of this Act what is in a person's best interests, the person making the determination must not make it merely on the basis of—*
   a. *the person's age or appearance, or*
   b. *a condition of his, or an aspect of his behaviour, which might lead others to make unjustified assumptions about what might be in his best interests.*

2) *The person making the determination must consider all the relevant circumstances and, in particular, take the following steps.*

3) [Section 3 omitted]

4) [Section 4 omitted]

5) *Where the determination relates to life-sustaining treatment he must not, in considering whether the treatment is in the best interests of the person concerned, be motivated by a desire to bring about his death.*

6) *He must consider, so far as is reasonably ascertainable—*
   a. *the person's past and present wishes and feelings (and, in particular, any relevant written statement made by him when he had capacity),*
   b. *the beliefs and values that would be likely to influence his decision if he had capacity, and*
   c. *the other factors that he would be likely to consider if he were able to do so.*

7) *He must take into account, if it is practicable and appropriate to consult them, the views of—*
   a. *anyone named by the person as someone to be consulted on the matter in question or on matters of that kind,*
   b. *anyone engaged in caring for the person or interested in his welfare,*
   c. *any donee [attorney]of a lasting power of attorney granted by the person, and*
   d. *any deputy appointed for the person by the court,*

*as to what would be in the person's best interests
and, in particular, as to the matters mentioned in
subsection 6.*

It would not be in a patient's best interests for them to receive a treatment that they have previously refused when they had the capacity to make a decision about that treatment.

As you will see in section 4 of the Mental Capacity Act 2005, relatives and carers have a role in assisting healthcare practitioners to determine the patient's wishes, beliefs, feelings and values to assist them in making the determination of what is in the patient's best interests. It is important to note that the role of relatives and carers is to assist the healthcare practitioners, not to make the determination of what the patient's best interests are. When a patient's best interests have been determined, the principle of necessity can be utilised to provide any treatment that is clinically necessary for the patient and is considered to be in their best interests.

Best interests can only be used to make treatment decisions for a patient when the patient lacks the capacity to make their own decisions and it is not possible to obtain consent from someone else. Best interests can be used for both child and adult patients.

As an aside, we have often been asked why the term is 'best interests' and not 'best interest'. This is related to the fact that a person has more than one interest. An individual may have a moral interest, a religious/spiritual interest, a physical interest, a psychological interest and a family interest. If only one interest was considered, for instance their physical interest, this would mean that important aspects of the individual's being and identity, and what they consider to be important in their life, would not be considered in the decision-making process for that individual.

As we did for a child in the section on *The child who lacks capacity to consent for themselves* above, considering what we have discussed in chapter 3 *Agreeing to treatment*, chapter 4 *Refusing* treatment, and this chapter, the following two lists show how consent can be provided, or refused for an adult, with regard to their healthcare needs:

Treatment can be authorised for an adult to meet their healthcare needs by:

- the adult themselves who has the capacity to make their own decision
- someone acting under a Lasting Power of Attorney for a patient who does not have the capacity to make their own decisions
- someone acting under the principle of necessity
- someone acting in the patient's best interests when they are unable to make their own treatment decisions

Treatment can be refused for an adult by:

- the adult themselves when they have the capacity to do so
- someone acting under a Lasting Power of Attorney for a patient who does not have the capacity to make their own decisions

Restriction of liberty

There are occasions when healthcare practitioners are faced with patients who, because of their current mental health status, are not able to make their own decisions about their mental health needs. This section discusses how these patients may have their liberty restricted and may be treated without their consent. It also considers what protections there are for patients who may be subject to compulsory detention and treatment.

There are other patients who are considered vulnerable because they are not able to consent for their own care and treatment because of a mental illness or a cognitive impairment and need to have their lives managed and so their liberty is restricted in some way to protect them. This section also considers these patients.

Mental health legislation

The purpose of mental health legislation is two-fold. It exists to provide a mechanism whereby patients who have a mental health disorder are able to receive treatment when they are unable to make a decision about their care and treatment due to their mental health disorder. This exists for the health and safety of the patient or for the protection of others.

The second reason for the existence of mental health legalisation is that it protects the rights of those patients who may need to be compulsorily detained to receive treatment or to compulsorily receive treatment against their will.

There are several main pieces of legislation that cover mental health in the United Kingdom. The main legislation is:

- Mental Health Act 1983 – this applies in full to England and Wales. Parts of the Act also apply to Northern Ireland and Scotland.
- The Mental Health (Northern Ireland) Order 1986, as amended by The Mental Health (Amendment) (Northern Ireland) Order 2004 is the main legislation for Northern Ireland.
- Mental Health (Care and Treatment) (Scotland) Act 2003 is the main legislation for Scotland

Mental health legislation does not just apply to adult patients. As an example, the Mental Health Act 1983 does not have a minimum age at which its provisions apply and so theoretically it could be applied to a very young child. Because of this, the legislations just listed all have provisions relating to children under 16 that provide guidance on how a child patient being detained or treated under its provisions should be dealt with compared to adult patients. Generally, these provide extra protections for the child patient, such as allowing parents to visit and more frequent reviews of their detention and/or treatment.

Detention and treatment under mental health legislation

As citizens of the United Kingdom, we have the right to liberty under Article 5 of the Human Rights Act 1998. This states that no-one should be deprived of their liberty without lawful reasons. There are exceptions to this, for instance those who have been convicted of a crime and sentenced to imprisonment. In all, there are six exceptions. The fifth includes the phrase 'person of unsound mind' (Article 5[1][e]). This means that those who are categorised as being of 'unsound mind' may lawfully have their liberty restricted. It is mental health legislation that provides the means by which this can happen, as well as the protection for the patient mentioned above.

A note on terminology. The language used to describe those who, in the words of the Human Rights Act 1998, are of 'unsound mind', can be problematic and emotive. We are going to use the term mental disorder as this is the term used in the Mental Health Act 1983, where it is defined as 'any disorder or disability of the mind' (Section 1[2]).

Rather than list all the various provisions in the legislation across the United Kingdom, we will use that from within the Mental Health Act 1983 as being indicative of the legislation in Northern Ireland and Scotland. Various provision exists within the Mental Health Act 1983 for the admission and treatment of individuals who have a mental disorder. Some of the main provisions relating to detention and treatment are:

- Section 2, which authorises the admission and detention of patients so that they can be assessed, for a period of up to 28 days
- Section 3, which allows a patient to be detained so that they can be treated, for a period of up to 6 months
- Section 4 allows for an emergency admission of up to 72 hours
- Section 5 is only used for patients who are already in hospital and allows them to be detained for a maximum of 72 hours so that they can be assessed to determine if they need treatment
- Section 7 authorises a patient aged 16 and over to be placed under a guardianship order. The effect of this is that it allows the patient to live outside of the hospital provided they follow certain restrictions such as living at a stated residence and attending for treatment.
- Section 20 allows those patients admitted under section 3 to have their detention extended. Initially this is for a period for 6 months, and then for a further year.

Because patients are admitted under a specific section of the legislation, colloquially they are known as 'being sectioned'. It is also possible for a patient with a mental disorder to admit themselves for an assessment or treatment of their mental disorder, or they agree to being admitted. Patients who admit themselves, or agree to their admission, are known as voluntary patients or informal patients, because they are not subject to a formal section.

Protection for the rights of patients who are compulsorily admitted or treated

Being subject to the provisions of mental health legislation means that an individual has their rights limited, including being treated without their consent and against their will. In order that their rights are affected as minimally as possible whilst still providing for their compulsory admission and treatment, mental health legislation has a series of protections in place.

Patients who are subject to the provision of mental health legislation have the following rights and protection:

- they cannot automatically be admitted, but formal processes have to be followed including that their admission needs to be recommended
- patients can only be admitted or treated against their will where the admission or treatment is recommended by two practitioners (this includes healthcare practitioners and social workers, one of whom has to have received specialist training and be approved to make the assessment).
- they can only be treated for their mental disorder against their will. They cannot be treated for a medical or surgical condition unrelated to their mental disorder just because they have been admitted under a section of mental health legislation. If treatment is needed for a medical or surgical condition, the consent of the patient is needed, unless the patient is under 16, when someone with parental responsibility may also provide consent.
- the relatives of the patient have a specified role, and rights and powers in relation to the patient. This is contained within mental health legislation and is discussed further in the next section.
- periods of admission are for a set maximum and whilst they can be extended, this can only be done on application and is not an automatic process.
- treatment is for set periods of time subject to a maximum period. As with admission, these periods can be extended but this can only be done on application and it not an automatic process.
- various individuals, such as hospital mangers, are required

to check on the patient's welfare and that their continued admission and treatment continues to be necessary.

- patients can apply to have their cases heard before a Mental Health Review Tribunal and ask to be discharged. The Mental Health Review Tribunal is required to assess if the reason for the patient to be admitted and treated still exists and if not, to discharge the patient.

℞ Role of relatives in mental health legislation

As discussed above and in chapter 2 *Engaging with healthcare*, mental health legislation, specifically the Mental Health Act 1983, allows relatives to perform specific roles and have defined rights and responsibilities when the patient is subject to mental health legislation provision, such as being detained for treatment. The term 'nearest relative' is generally used when talking about relatives and mental health legislation and healthcare.

Some of the roles a 'nearest relative' may perform include:

- applying for the patient to be assessed for their mental health condition
- applying for the patient to be admitted for treatment of their mental health condition
- applying for the patient to be placed under a guardianship order, which would mean that a guardian is appointed for the patient and may make some decisions on behalf of the patient who is unable to do so themselves.

Essentially, these applications are to a relevant authority to request that the patient receives appropriate treatment when the patient is unable to do so themselves, because of their mental health condition. The 'nearest relative' also has roles in relation to receiving information about the patient and their treatment and can object to the patient being detained and apply to have the patient discharged from their detention.

The reason that the Mental Health Act 1983 has a 'nearest relative' provision is to allow for an individual to focus on the best interests of the patient and to act as an advocate for them whilst the patient is unable to do so.

Under section 26(1) of the Mental Health Act 1983, the nearest relative is the person highest in the following list (if there is more than one person in a category, it is generally the oldest of them who would be considered the nearest relative):

1. *husband or wife or civil partner* (also includes someone who has been living with the patient for a period of not less than 6 months as the patient's husband, wife, or civil partner unless the patient already has a husband, wife or civil partner)
2. *son or daughter independent*
3. *father or mother*
4. *brother or sister*
5. *grandparent*
6. *grandchild*
7. *uncle or aunt*
8. *nephew or niece*

Patients are able to request that someone other than the person recognised as the 'nearest relative' is appointed instead. Also, a person identified as the 'nearest relative' may refuse to take on the role and request that someone else is appointed to the role.

The role of the 'nearest relative' acts as an additional protection for those patients who are subject to compulsory admission and treatment. Ideally, the patient and their 'nearest relative' will have a close relationship that enables the patient to receive the support they need as well as having an advocate who can speak for them when they are unable to do so themselves.

If the patient is a child, it is expected that their parent will fulfil the function of the 'nearest relative'.

Protecting vulnerable patients and their liberty

There are some patients who lack the capacity to make decisions for themselves to an extent that they need to be cared for to ensure that they do not come to harm. It is possible to see these patients as being vulnerable because they are reliant upon others for their care needs.

Surprisingly, given that both the Mental Capacity Act 2005 and the Mental Health Act 1983 have provisions that protect individuals from being exploited and ensure that their rights are upheld, neither have a legal definition of what a vulnerable person is. For our discussion, a vulnerable patient is one who lacks the capacity to make decisions regarding their care needs and requires high levels of care, including supervision, to ensure that they remain safe.

There are various reasons why a vulnerable patient may lack the capacity to make their own care decisions:

- age
- cognitive disorders
- developmental learning disability
- emotional disorder
- mental illness
- mental impairment
- physical condition causing cognitive impairment
- physical or mental dependency

Vulnerable patients should receive treatment in their best interests. Because they are not able to care for themselves, the care and treatment they receive will usually result in them having their liberty restricted by a need for them to live in care homes or hospital. For instance, it may be in the best interest of a patient who lacks the capacity to make their own decisions and is unable to care for themselves to reside in a care home where their needs can be met.

Some patients may be compliant with their accommodation arrangements, even if they have not made the decision themselves, whilst others may want to leave, even though they lack the capacity to make decisions and are unable to care for themselves. In both of these situations, residing in a care home can be seen as a form of restriction of the vulnerable patient's liberty, as they did not choose to reside in the care home.

Ordinarily, a patient who has their liberty restricted would have this done under mental health legislation because they are being assessed or treated for their mental disorder. As a vulnerable patient is not being treated for their mental disorder, as defined by mental health legislation, they will not come under the protection afforded by mental health legislation and so would not have any formal protection in place to act as a safeguard against unwarranted restriction of their liberty.

Recognising that there were a group of vulnerable patients who fell between having full liberty and having their liberty restricted under the protection of mental health legislation, and because of a number of legal challenges to the restriction of individual vulnerable patients, a range of safeguards were introduced to act as a form of protection for these patients.

It was the Mental Health Act 2007 that introduced Deprivation of Liberty Safeguards (DoLS) by amending the Mental Capacity Act 2005. Deprivation of Liberty Safeguards are a system of protections that are used to ensure that arrangements for vulnerable patients are based around their best interests, and that any restrictions on their liberty are the minimum needed to ensure their safety. DoLS also allow for the restriction of liberty to be assessed to determine if it is necessary and where a restriction of liberty is authorised, for the restriction to be reviewed and challenged.

DoLS requires that before a restriction of a vulnerable person's liberty is authorised:

- The assessment of whether the vulnerable patient can have their liberty restricted has to be undertaken by two independent assessors
- One independent assessor is a mental health assessor, the other is a best interests assessor
- Both assessors must have received training for their role
- Six separate assessments have to take place before a deprivation of a vulnerable patient's liberty is authorised under DoLS. These are that the vulnerable patient has to:
  o be 18 or over
  o be suffering from a mental disorder
  o lack capacity to make decisions for themselves including about the restriction of their liberty
  o have the restrictions placed on them in their best interests, to allow them to receive appropriate care
  o be unable to be detained under mental health legislation
  o not have an advance decision in place that has refused the care, or not to have an LPA that refuses the care, or have an attorney who has previously refused the care or the restriction of their liberty

If the restriction of the vulnerable patient's liberty is authorised this can be for up to one year. An authorisation cannot usually be extended but a new assessment can be made for up to another 12 months.

The protections in place under DoLS for a vulnerable patient include:

- Consultation with relatives, carers and friends as part of the assessment process
- Independent representatives who advocate for the vulnerable person.
- Regular reviews of the deprivation of liberty to assess if it is still needed

- An ability to challenge the deprivation of liberty through the Court of Protection. This can be done either by the vulnerable patient or by their independent representative.

Deprivation of Liberty Safeguards are due to be replaced by Liberty Protection Safeguards (LPS). A major change with LPS as opposed to DoLS is that LPS will apply to everyone over the age of 16, as DoLS only applies to those aged 18 and over. Other changes that LPS will introduce are:

- A simplified legal framework
- They will apply to vulnerable patients in supported accommodation. DoLS only applies to those in care homes and hospitals
- DoLS only apply to a single specific residence for the vulnerable patient. LPS will enable the vulnerable patient to be able to move between residences as their circumstances change.
- The time limits that the safeguard puts in place will change, so that it can be up to a year initially and then renewed on application for a further year, with subsequent applications allowing for renewal for up to three years at a time, depending upon the vulnerable patient's circumstances not changing.

LPS were initially scheduled to replace DoLS in October 2020. At the time of writing, the government have announced that LPS will be delayed for this parliament at least, which could run until the end of 2024. Any decision around implementing LPS would then need to be made by the next elected government.

CHAPTER 6

CONFIDENTIALITY

This chapter looks at confidentiality, also known in healthcare as clinical confidentiality. It starts by considering what confidentiality is and the need for confidentiality in healthcare. This leads into a discussion on how ethics and the law support confidentiality in healthcare and an examination of the duty of confidentiality that healthcare practitioners have.

This is followed by an examination of what confidential information is, how confidentiality can be maintained in healthcare, how confidential information may be lawfully shared, and with whom. There is consideration of sharing information in the public interest and the sharing of information with relatives.

Chapter 6 then moves on to explore the actions a patient could take if their confidentiality was breached.

The difference between a child and an adult patient in relation to confidentiality is considered, as well as confidentiality after the death of a patient.

Health records and their purpose is discussed before an examination of how patients can access their own health records, as well as the accessing of health records by relatives. Chapter 6 concludes by discussing visiting patients in hospital.

Confidentiality in healthcare

Confidentiality can be thought of as shorthand for keeping things private. In healthcare, practitioners will refer to 'clinical confidentiality', where the 'things' to be kept private are the patient's information. The purpose of maintaining confidentiality is to ensure that information that is considered to be private is not shared beyond those individuals who need access to that information for the purposes of assisting and treating the patient.

The reason for confidentiality

It has already been stated several times in this book that information is key to healthcare. Healthcare practitioners need information from patients in order to be able to assist them in meeting their healthcare needs. Because of the nature of healthcare, some of this information will be of a private nature. Because it is private to them, patients will want to keep the information private and not have it freely shared but to limit its sharing.

If patients were not willing to share their personal information because they feared it would be made freely available, it could make a healthcare practitioner's job impossible. It is also possible that patients who feared their personal information being misused or shared widely would not seek the assistance of healthcare practitioners. This would mean that patients would not have their healthcare needs met and the patients and others who are affected by their state of health will suffer.

If we consider who could be affected by the ill-health of an individual patient, it could include, amongst others:

- Spouses and partners
- Children
- Those dependent upon them
- Other relatives
- Friends
- Employers

- Work colleagues
- Customers and clients of their employer

Quite a lot of people could be affected by a patient not being able to fulfil their family or professional role if they were ill. Therefore, there needs to be a mechanism by which patients are assured that the information that they give to healthcare practitioners as part of their healthcare will be kept private and not freely shared or misused. They will then be more likely to seek help to meet any healthcare needs they have.

This is the role of confidentiality; it ensures that the trust between patients and their healthcare practitioners is maintained by protecting private information and, in so doing, encourages individuals to seek assistance in meeting their healthcare needs. Additionally, having personal information kept confidential means that the flow of information between patient and healthcare practitioner is continued. Thus, healthcare practitioners should have the information they need to provide appropriate assistance and treatment to their patients.

Confidentiality as a patient right

Patients have a legal right to confidentiality in their interactions with healthcare practitioners. This means that if their confidentiality has been breached, that is their information has been shared without lawful reason, they can take legal action against those who shared their personal information. There are some specific times when confidentiality can be breached, and these are discussed below.

Ethics, law and confidentiality

Both ethics and law support the maintenance of confidentiality in healthcare interactions.

Confidentiality as an ethical principle of healthcare practice has been around for a very long time. It is a part of the Hippocratic Oath which dates to around 300 – 200 BC, where there is mention of not divulging information gained in the course of acting as a practitioner but instead keeping such things secret.

Ethically, confidentially is related to the principle of autonomy; that a patient has the autonomy to decide who has access to their personal information and should be allowed to manage this themselves. After all, it is the patient themselves who knows what information they consider to be personal and needing to be kept confidential and which information they are happy to have freely shared.

Legally, there is no one single source of law on confidentiality. Rather, confidentiality arises in both common law and statute, and not just one statue either. Some of the statutory provisions which deal with confidentiality include:

- Data Protection Act 2018, which gives individuals control over their data (personal information)
- Health and Social Care Act 2012, which has provisions about how personal information is dealt with, including a requirement for certain personal information to be recorded
- Human Rights Act 1998, which provides a right in relation to respect for private and family life
- Official Secrets Act 1989, though not in relation to healthcare!

Although unfortunately there is no one law that we could visit to read all about the law of confidentiality, legal protection exists to keep personal information confidential. This legal protection is based on the right to privacy.

As a side note: the Freedom of Information Act 2000 does not cover personal information and so cannot be used to see the information that a public authority holds about you. If you want to see the information an organisation holds about you, you should use the subject access provisions in the Data Protection Act 2018 for this.

The duty of confidentiality

As well as the legal protection that exists to keep a patient's personal information confidential, healthcare practitioners are under a duty of confidentiality. This duty of confidentiality arises from two main sources.

All healthcare practitioners who are employed will have a contract of employment. This contract of employment will, amongst other things, clearly spell out the healthcare practitioner's duty in respect of keeping information that they receive as part of their role confidential. A healthcare practitioner's failure to maintain their contractual duty of confidentiality can see them face disciplinary action from their employer and/or regulator.

Not all healthcare practitioners are employed. Some may be self-employed and then will not have a contract of employment. However, all healthcare practitioners who are registered with one of the healthcare practitioner regulators (see chapter 2 *Engaging with healthcare* for a discussion and explanation of healthcare practitioner regulators), are subject to the codes of conduct that the regulator issues to them.

These codes of conduct all have a provision which imposes a duty of confidentiality on the healthcare practitioner that requires them to keep patient information confidential. If a healthcare practitioner breaches their duty under their code of conduct, they could face a fitness to practise investigation by their regulator, and if found to have failed to maintain the standard required, because they did not keep their patient's information confidential, could ultimately be removed from the regulator's register and not be able to practise their profession.

Finally, the duty of confidentiality arises for healthcare practitioners in NHS Codes of Confidentiality which apply to all those who work in the NHS.

Caldicott Guardians

In your healthcare interactions you may come across the term Caldicott Guardians. Since 1998, it has been a legal requirement that every NHS organisation has a Caldicott Guardian. They are someone in a senior position in the organisation who has the responsibility of ensuring that the organisation complies with all legal and regulatory requirements relating to the use of personal information that the organisation has about its patients. They oversee how confidential information is managed within the organisation and the arrangements for sharing of information both within the organisation and with external agencies. Since 2002, social care organisations have also been required to have Caldicott Guardians. In short, Caldicott Guardians advise their organisation on how to maintain the confidentiality of patient information. Individuals within the organisation can also seek guidance from the Caldicott Guardian on issues relating to confidential information in specific cases.

Confidential information

So far in this chapter, we have referred to personal information and private information and the patient's right to confidentiality. Now, not all of a patient's personal information needs to be kept confidential. Indeed, not all patient information can be kept confidential.

Let's take a moment and consider what information may be confidential and what may not.

Many legal cases have considered if a particular set of

information should be classified as confidential and therefore subject to the law on confidentiality and be protected from being passed on.

From two of these cases, we can determine that:

- Information of a personal and intimate nature is confidential – this was determined in Stephens v Avery [1998] which concerned someone informing a national newspaper of their 'friend's' sexual relationships.
- A person's private life is confidential – this was determined in Campbell v MGN Limited [2004] which was to consider if a newspaper could publish information about a model's private life.

Therefore, anything that is related to a person's private life or that is of a personal and intimate nature can be considered confidential information and fall under the law of confidentiality and need to be protected.

Two other legal cases help us consider if specific information should be treated as confidential information or not.

Coco v Clark [1968] was concerned with the disclosure of high value technical information, whilst Attorney-General v Guardian Newspapers (No. 2) [1990] was concerned with whether a former member of the United Kingdom's secret service could publish their memoirs. Two main points emerge from these cases in relation to confidential information. These are:

- How the information is divulged is important in considering if the information should be classified as confidential or not
- If the information is already in the public arena, it cannot be confidential

Taken together, this means that there is a further factor regarding whether information should be classed as being confidential or not. This relates to the circumstances of how information was originally shared and if it is already known.

From what we have seen so far, the law considers that confidential information includes personal and/or intimate information and information about a person's private life, but the circumstances of how it was originally divulged and whether it is already available to the public will affect whether it should be treated as being confidential. An example may help us with determine whether information should be classified as confidential or not.

If a patient provides personal information to a healthcare practitioner in a consultation where only the patient and the healthcare practitioner is present, most people will probably see this as a private conversation. If, on the other hand, the patient shares exactly the same information on national television during a live broadcast about healthcare, most people would not see this a private conversation.

The former is information that has a personal nature about it, is not already known to the public (we do not know otherwise so let's assume it isn't) and is given to the healthcare practitioner in a way that most of us would consider private. This information would therefore be seen as needing to be protected as confidential information.

On the other hand, while the patient disclosing information to the public on live television is also talking about information of a personal nature, and it is probably not already known to the public, the way in which they have passed on the information does not imply that they expected it to be kept private. Therefore, this information would not be protected as confidential information. In fact, it would be impossible to keep this confidential as anyone and everyone who watched the television broadcast would know the information.

From the above it can be seen that from a strictly legal perspective, where information is already known outside of the healthcare team there is no duty of confidentiality for that piece of information.

However, because of the healthcare practitioner's duty of confidentiality, healthcare practitioners are held to a higher standard and have to keep all patient information confidential, even if it could be said to be already known to a third party (that is someone who is not the patient or a member of the healthcare team). This means that a patient's personal information can only be divulged by healthcare practitioners in limited situations, which are discussed in the next section.

If it is not one of the situations discussed below, your healthcare practitioner has to keep your personal information confidential.

Sharing confidential information

Healthcare practitioners, it has been said several times in this book, need patient information in order to be able to effectively care for and treat them. We have also acknowledged that healthcare practitioners generally work within a team and various members of the team will need access to the patient's information in order to be able to provide their part of the patient's care and treatment.

Yet, this chapter has so far all been about maintaining the confidentiality of patient information, and it has been said that healthcare practitioners have to maintain the confidentiality of the information that their patients give them. This raises the issue of how healthcare practitioners can uphold their legal and regulatory responsibilities concerning their patient's personal information, and at the same time work within a healthcare team and ensure that patients receive the care and treatment they need.

▣ Healthcare practitioners and the sharing of information amongst members of the healthcare team

It would be no surprise that you would want the best possible care and treatment from your healthcare practitioners. Because it is recognised that you would want this, it is considered that you are willing to allow all members of the healthcare team to have access to the information necessary to provide you with the care and treatment you need.

In a departure from the usual legal position that your personal information has to be kept confidential, the legal and ethical position is that it is in your best interests for your confidential information to be shared amongst the members of the healthcare team who are caring for and treating you. This is achieved through the principle of implied consent discussed in chapter 3 *Agreeing to treatment*. Unlike other instances of treatment where you need to provide your consent, in relation to your information, by accepting treatment it is implied that you are consenting for your information to be shared amongst those members of the healthcare team who need it.

There are still some protections in place to keep your personal information as confidential as possible, whilst allowing access to those members of the healthcare team who need it. Firstly, the members of the healthcare team who are allowed to access your information under the presumption of implied consent are only those who are caring for you or treating you. If a healthcare practitioner who is not involved in your care or treatment were to access your personal information, this would constitute a breach of confidentiality.

Secondly, just because a healthcare practitioner is part of the healthcare team who are providing your care and treatment does not mean that they can just go and freely access your personal information. There has to be a genuine clinical need for them to access it. Healthcare practitioners who need access to your personal information should only access that part of your personal information which is needed for the particular role they are providing in your overall care and treatment. If a healthcare practitioner were to access information that they did not need, this could constitute a breach of confidentiality.

Finally, if a healthcare practitioner who has a genuine need for your personal information were to access it and then share it with another healthcare practitioner who is not a member of your healthcare team, that practitioner would be breaching your confidentiality.

Whilst the assumption of you giving implied consent to members of the healthcare team who are caring for and treating you is ethically and legally recognised, and accepted as part of healthcare, it is limited in its scope and works for your best interests.

Aside from sharing information with other healthcare practitioners involved in the care and treatment of the patient, there are three other main ways in which a patient's confidential information may be shared. These are when:

- the patient gives consent for it to be shared
- it is in the patient's best interests
- the public interest demands it

Patient consent for information to be shared

The consent of the patient for information to be shared is the primary way of ensuring ethical and legal justification is present when sharing information. If you give consent to a healthcare practitioner to share your personal information, that healthcare practitioner cannot breach your confidentiality, unless they go outside of the bounds of information sharing for which you gave consent.

This is why you may find healthcare practitioners ask you about sharing your information with other members of the healthcare team, and more widely if necessary, and ask you for permission (consent) to do so. It means that they can ensure they are acting in your best interests, and that they cannot breach your confidentiality and so cannot breach their employer's rules or their regulator's code of conduct.

As with any consent, it must be voluntary consent from you, and you should not be under pressure to provide your consent. If you did provide your consent to the sharing of your information under duress or undue pressure, this would not be a legally valid consent, and so no consent would exist.

As with any consent for any other aspect of healthcare, consent can only be given by a competent patient and so patients not deemed to be competent will not be able to give consent for their information to be shared. Likewise, if the patient is a child, they can give their own consent if they are over 16 but need to be assessed as Gillick competent in relation to the sharing of their information if they are under 16.

Someone with parental responsibility is also able to provide consent on behalf of a child over 16 who refuses to give their own consent, or for a child under 16 not considered to be Gillick competent. Gillick competence is explored in chapter 3 *Agreeing to treatment.*

Patient best interests for information to be shared

Information can be shared in a patient's best interests when the patient is not able to provide consent themselves. Using best interests as a justification for sharing a patient's information is not a way of circumventing a situation where a patient won't consent but is able to do so, that is a patient who is refusing to give their consent to the sharing of their information.

Another way that best interests can be used in the sharing of information is where a healthcare practitioner has a reason to suspect that a patient is being abused or neglected.

If the patient is competent to make their own decisions, the healthcare practitioner who suspects that they are being abused or neglected can offer assistance and advice to the patient but needs to be careful how they use that information. They could share it with a more senior member of the healthcare team for their guidance, but they are not allowed to share the information with third parties without the patient's consent.

However, if the patient is not competent to make a decision about this themselves, the healthcare practitioner is legally allowed to share that information with a third party in the best interests of the patient. The healthcare practitioner's legal duty of confidentiality is overthrown by their duty to their patient and their wellbeing.

If a healthcare practitioner were to use the information they have without a patient's consent, they need to ensure that they report their concerns to an appropriate third party. In this case, that would be someone who is able to act on it to protect the patient, such as the police or social services, and not a friend or the media. The healthcare practitioner also has to ensure that they provide the minimum amount of information that is necessary to allow the third party to act but will not disclose personal patient information that is unnecessary and so breach the patient's confidentiality further than needed.

Public interest in sharing confidential information

So far in this chapter it has been the best interests of the patient that have been paramount when considering confidential information and when that information can be shared. The ethical and legal position in sharing a patient's personal information starts with the assumption that a patient's information will be held to be confidential unless there is an overriding public interest reason why this should not be the case.

We should point out that a balance has to be achieved

between disclosing patient information for a public interest reason and the overarching public interest in maintaining the confidentiality of patient information as discussed in *The reason for confidentiality*. It is also worth noting that there is a difference between what is in the public interest and what the public may be interested in knowing about. As we will see there are some significant public interest reasons why a patient's personal information should be shared without their consent, as opposed to sharing patient information because the public may be interested in knowing about their favourite television or sports personality's health information.

Public interest reasons for the sharing of confidential patient information include:

- Protecting third parties from harm – it is in the public interest to protect individuals from a known harm, even if this means that an individual's personal information may need to be breached to achieve this. The individuals that are protected include children and vulnerable adults who may be subject to alleged abuse or neglect, either from the patient or from those known to the patient. It also includes individuals who the patient may intend to harm and who need to be warned about the risk from the patient to allow them to take the necessary action to protect themselves.
- Prevention of crime and in police investigations – it is in the public interest that the police are able to fully investigate crime and crimes are prevented or solved. Whilst it is not the role of healthcare practitioners to act as police assistants, if the healthcare practitioner has information that may prevent a crime that is considered to be of a grave and serious nature, they have the legal authority to share that information with an appropriate authority.
- Because of a statutory requirement – it is in the public

interest that healthcare practitioners fulfil their statutory requirements. There are several Acts of Parliament which require healthcare practitioners to provide patient information to a relevant authority, for instance, the Misuse of Drugs Act 1971, the Road Traffic Act 1988, and the Terrorism Act 2000.

- Public health reasons – it is in the public interest that the health of the public is maintained and any threats to public health are removed or minimised. If a patient has a disease that is highly infectious and will not accept treatment or isolate themselves, the healthcare practitioner can lawfully inform the relevant authority of the patient and their details so that the risk from the patient to the public is identified and can be dealt with appropriately.
- On the order of a court – it is in the public interest that instructions from a court are followed. A court can order any confidential information to be supplied to it and these do not just have to be for any of the public interest reasons mentioned above.

Where there is a public interest reason for a patient's personal information to be shared without the patient's consent, only the minimum amount of information which meets the reason for the disclosure of that information should be shared.

Anonymised information

Where a patient's personal information is anonymised, so that it is not possible to identify a patient from that information, that information can be lawfully used for audit and research purposes without breaching a patient's confidentiality.

૪ Sharing confidential information with relatives

Generally, there is no right for relatives to be given a patient's confidential information. Confidential information may be shared with relatives with the patient's consent. If the patient is not able to consent, healthcare practitioners may share information with relatives where they believe that doing so is in the best interests of the patient. It can be argued that informing a relative who telephones a healthcare centre and asks if the patient is in fact a patient there is in the patient's best interests, unless the patient has expressly stated they do not want a relative to be told of their presence. This is because if the relative was not informed that the patient was present in the healthcare centre, the relative may worry about where the patient is.

If an individual exercises parental responsibility for a child (see chapter 3 *Agreeing to treatment*), as part of that process they will need appropriate confidential information. It is important to note that parents do not have a right to confidential information where a child has given their own consent, either because they are over 16 or they are assessed as being Gillick competent.

Other than with the patient's consent or in their best interests if they are unable to provide their consent, sharing the patient's information with a relative would constitute a breach of the patient's confidentiality.

Breach of confidentiality

If a patient's personal information has been unlawfully shared this is known as a breach of confidence. If a patient believes that their confidence has been breached, whether intentionally or not, they have several avenues of action they can take.

An unintentional breach of the patient's information would include a situation where the healthcare practitioner has been careless with patient information. Examples of this would be leaving the patient's notes in a place where someone not authorised has access to them and can read them.

An intentional breach of patient information would include situations such as where a healthcare practitioner contacts a newspaper and shares personal healthcare information about a television personality in exchange for money.

Complaints

The patient can make a complaint to the healthcare organisation which held their personal data and ask them to investigate. If a breach is found to have occurred, this could result in disciplinary action against any individuals involved.

If the patient is aware that a specific healthcare practitioner(s) has unlawfully shared their personal information, they can make a complaint directly to the healthcare practitioner's regulator and ask them to investigate and take any appropriate action against the healthcare practitioner(s).

Legal action

The patient can also take legal action against a healthcare practitioner who has breached their confidence and/or a healthcare provider. This would involve the patient suing the healthcare practitioner and/or healthcare provider. The patient would have to prove that they have suffered a loss as a result of the disclosure of their personal information and that it was the healthcare practitioner and/or healthcare provider who was responsible for the breach of confidentiality. As it is not possible to make information confidential again once it has been disclosed, the patient would receive damages, an award of money as compensation, if they won their case.

Potential breach of confidentiality

If the breach of confidentiality has not yet occurred but the patient has concerns that their personal information is going to be shared, whether intentionally or not, they have several potential courses of action.

The patient can raise their concerns with their healthcare practitioner and ask them to take action to ensure that their confidential information is secure. If the patient's concern is about their healthcare practitioner, they can ask to speak to a manager and raise it with them.

Alternatively, the patient can apply to the courts for an injunction. An injunction is a legal means of preventing something happening. In this situation, the injunction would order the healthcare practitioner and/or the healthcare provider not to disclose the patient's personal information on penalty of legal sanction.

✍ Healthcare practitioners who breach a patient's confidentiality

If a healthcare practitioner breaches a patient's confidentiality, whether intentionally or not, they could face disciplinary action from their employer or from their regulator.

The employer could impose a sanction, ranging from requiring them to retrain on the principles of confidentiality and the handling of patient information, to a suspension, or for the most serious of cases dismissal of the healthcare practitioner from their employment.

The healthcare practitioner's regulator has a similar range of sanctions, including

- a requirement to retrain on the handling of patient information and confidentiality
- requiring that the healthcare practitioner does not work

with patient information for a set period of time or until them have completed any retraining,

- suspension from the register for a set period of time, which means that the healthcare practitioner cannot work as a registered healthcare practitioner during the period of their suspension
- removing the healthcare practitioner from the register, meaning that the healthcare practitioner can never work as a registered healthcare practitioner regulated by that particular regulator.

The child and confidentiality

As we know from chapter 3 *Agreeing to treatment*, legally a child is anyone under the age of 18. A child patient has a legal right to confidentiality in a similar way that an adult patient does and has legal protections regarding their personal information.

There are, however, some differences between the child patient and the adult patient when considering the confidentiality of their personal information. These differences relate to two main areas: providing consent for the sharing of personal information and taking action in relation to a breach of confidentiality or a suspected breach.

In chapter 3 the rights of a child were discussed in relation to consent. It was noted that legally, child patients can be classified into one of two groups; those under sixteen, and those 16 or 17. The role of the parent and parental responsibility was also discussed.

Because of the law on child patients giving their own consent, a child's personal information is only confidential when they are either over 16 or if they are assessed as being Gillick competent. A patient who is under 16 and not classed as being Gillick competent is not able to provide their own consent, and this applies to confidential information as well.

This is due to the fact that the child patient, under 16 and not assessed as being Gillick competent, does not possess the legal right to have their personal healthcare information withheld from someone with parental responsibility for them. This is so that the person with parental responsibility has all the relevant information on which to base any treatment decisions they need to make on behalf of the child.

A person with parental responsibility can provide consent for a child's personal healthcare information to be shared, without agreement from the child, and can even override a child's refusal to provide consent if the child is Gillick competent or over 16.

The other difference between a child patient and an adult patient is that a child patient is not able to act in relation to a suspected breach or an actual breach of their confidentiality. Until they reach the age of 18, someone with parental responsibility would have to initiate a formal complaint or start any legal action on their behalf.

⚡ Confidentiality when the patient has died

When a patient dies, a healthcare practitioner's duty of confidentiality continues to survive the death of their patient. This means that all of the discussion regarding confidentiality in this chapter still applies, and information that was protected as confidential information when the patient was alive will continue to be protected as confidential information.

Relatives of the patient do not have any right to request that the patient's confidential information is passed to them. As we saw above, if a relative was to ask for confidential information about the patient when the patient is alive, the healthcare practitioner would ask the patient what they wanted them to do and if they give consent for the information to be passed to the relative. If, when alive, the patient was not able to give consent, a decision would be made as to whether it was in the patient's best interests for the relative to have the information. Information is only given to relatives when the patient gives their consent, or where the patient is incompetent with regard to consent, it is considered by their healthcare practitioner to be in their best interests for the information being requested be shared with their relatives.

Obviously, a patient who has died is unable to provide their consent for information to be shared with their relatives. This means that the information can only be shared on the basis of the best interests of the patient.

If a patient had left instructions, whilst alive, that their information is not to be given to their relatives, the healthcare practitioner would be able to use this to keep the information confidential.

If there are no instructions from the patient regarding their personal information, the healthcare practitioner has to balance what they know about the patient against the request for information from the relatives. This would include a consideration of whether releasing the information to the relatives would be a benefit to them or would cause them distress, and if releasing the information would change the relative's perception of the patient.

Other ways in which a patient's information may be released after their death are in relation to the death certificate, where the disclosure is required by law, or it is requested by a coroner or in relation to a coroner's inquest.

Breach of confidentiality after the death of the patient

As noted above in *Breach of confidentiality,* if a patient believes that their confidentiality has been breached, they can make a complaint to the NHS organisation where they received their care or treatment, the healthcare practitioner's regulator, or they can seek damages through the courts.

After the death of the patient, it is the estate of the patient that can act in relation to a breach of the patient's confidential information or to prevent information being released. If the patient's estate is taking legal action it would have to demonstrate that it has suffered a loss, for an actual breach, or would suffer a loss, to prevent a breach.

The situation with regard to a patient's health records after the death of the patient is discussed below in *Health records after the patient has died.*

Health records

The Data Protection Act 2018, in section 205[1], provides a useful definition of what a healthcare record is:

'Health record' means a record which

(a) consists of data concerning health, and

(b) has been made by or on behalf of a health professional in connection with the diagnosis, care or treatment of the individual to whom the data relates'

A health record may be in paper format or held electronically, or a combination of both.

Health records contain all the information about your health and your healthcare episodes and the care and treatment you have received. Ideally, you would have one health record that was complete and up to date. However, given that you are likely to have lived in several places throughout your lifetime and have received healthcare from various healthcare organisations and healthcare practitioners, it is possible that you have several different health records.

For the purposes of examining your rights in relation to your health records, we will include any and all of your health records as if they were one single set.

Your health record may include:

- Information about you such as your date of birth, address, your health episodes to date, any allergies you may have, any current medications you take, details of your next of kin
- Notes your GP has made about your consultations with them
- Letter of referral from your GP to specialist healthcare practitioners
- Results of tests you have received
- Consent forms you may have signed
- Notes about treatment you have received
- Observation by healthcare practitioners about you and your healthcare needs and response to any care and/or treatment you have received
- Letters from specialist healthcare practitioners to your GP informing them of any care and treatment you have received

Health records exist to allow healthcare practitioners to have access to information they need to ensure that your healthcare needs are met. This is why they are intended to be a complete record of your health and healthcare interactions. Healthcare practitioners also use your health records to communicate with each other about your health and the healthcare needs you have, and their plans for your care and treatment. By having all the information in your health record, any healthcare practitioner should be able to continue your care and treatment.

Health records can also be used to plan healthcare services in geographical areas and to assess how effective certain treatments are. This is through audit and research such as statistical analysis of a large numbers of health records. When used in this way, the health records will be anonymised so the auditors and researchers do not have details of the patient's personal details in full, so they could not identify a specific person from the information they have.

You do not own your own health record. For NHS patients, the health record is owned by the Secretary of State for Health. In reality, they are held and maintained by individual NHS organisations in the name of the Secretary of State for Health. If the patient is under the care of a private, non-NHS healthcare practitioner, their health record will be owned by either the healthcare practitioner themselves if they are self-employed, or by the organisation that employs the healthcare practitioner.

Accessing health records

Your health record can legitimately be accessed by any healthcare practitioner who is involved in your care and treatment and needs the information to be able to provide that care and treatment.

Although you do not own your own health record, many patients believe that they do. Because of this, they also believe that they have a right to access their health record whenever they want. This is not true. You do not have the right to access or read your health record whenever you want. You may actually have your health record in your hands, but even that doesn't give you the right to read them and you could be asked to return them if you were seen to be reading them!

The reason you do not have an automatic right to your health record is for your benefit. It is because your health record may contain the results of tests and investigations that are written to allow them to be used by other healthcare practitioners and this may not be clear to you or us. If you have questions about your care and treatment, you should ask your healthcare practitioner so that they can explain and discuss any findings from tests and investigations.

Accessing your own health record

If you want to read your own health record, you need to request access to it. There are different rights and ways of doing this depending upon your reason for accessing your health record.

If you just want to access your health record, the Data Protection Act 2018 gives you the right to do so. The Act also gives you the right to have any inaccurate information corrected. There is no fee for making an access request under the Data Protection Act 2018.

If you are considering bringing a legal case for negligence in respect of any aspect of your healthcare, you can apply to the High Court under the Supreme Court Act 1981 for access to the relevant part of your health record. The High Court does not have to provide access and generally will only do so where they believe that a claim for negligence will actually occur.

If the reason you want to see your health record is because a health report is being requested as part of an insurance claim or as part of an employment process, the Access to Medical Reports Act 1988 gives you the right to do this. The Act also gives you the right to have any inaccuracies corrected, or to add a note to the report to explain some aspect of it. You also have the right to stop the report being sent to the insurer or prospective employer.

Exemptions to accessing your health record

Although, as just discussed, you have legal rights to access your own health record, there are two main exemptions where you will not be given access to the record or to parts of it. The first exemption is where there is reasonable belief that accessing your health record or a specific part of it would cause you, or somebody else, serious physical or mental harm. The second exemption is where information about a third person would be disclosed to you.

If either or both of the exemptions applies to you, you may either have the whole of your health record withheld or you may have the relevant part of the health record withheld. You should be told if there is a part of your health record withheld from you.

Child health records

A child aged 16 or over or assessed as being Gillick competent may apply for access to their own health record. A parent or other person with parental responsibility may also apply for access to their child's health record.

⚘ Accessing your relative's health record

There is no automatic right to access your relative's health record, although there are three ways you can gain access.

The first is if your relative will give their consent to you accessing their health record.

The second way is if your relative is not able to give their own consent and you have a Lasting Power of Attorney (which is discussed in chapter 5 *When the patient lacks the capacity to consent for their own healthcare needs*) in relation to their health needs. The final way you may access the health record of a relative also occurs when the patient is unable to give or withhold their consent. If a healthcare practitioner believes that it is in the patient's best interests for you to have access to their health record, you may be granted access.

If you are granted access to the health record of a relative, you may not be granted full access but only be allowed to access the part relevant to a specific healthcare episode. Parts may also be withheld if it would identify another person, or it is considered that it would cause significant harm to you or another person's physical or mental health.

Requesting healthcare practitioners not to make an entry in your health record

There are times when you may want to have a discussion with a healthcare practitioner but not want a record made of the discussion. If this is a situation you find yourself in, you need to raise this at the beginning of the discussion as the healthcare practitioner may agree not to record the discussion but equally, they may tell you that they are not prepared to do this. Alternatively, they may agree not to record full details but will still need to make a short entry in your health record.

The reason why a healthcare practitioner may not agree to have an off-the-record discussion with you is because they consider the discussion will be relevant to your future health-care needs and other healthcare practitioners may need to be aware of it.

⏁ Healthcare practitioners and health records

As noted earlier, healthcare practitioners who are involved in your care and treatment and need the information in your health record to be able to provide that care and treatment, can access them.

However, healthcare practitioners cannot lawfully access their own health records without going through the same application for access as you or any other patient. Because the only lawful reason that a healthcare practitioner can access someone's health record is in order to care and treat them, they cannot access the health record of a relative or a friend, unless they are caring for or treating them.

If a healthcare practitioner were to access their own or a relative's or friend's health record without lawful reason, they would potentially be facing disciplinary action from their employer, and an investigation by their regulator.

Health records after the patient has died

After the death of a patient, the confidential status of their health record continues. This means that access to it is still restricted.

If a relative wants to access the health record of a patient who has died, they cannot apply under the Data Protection Act 2018 as this only applies to living people. However, the Access to Health Records Act 1990 provides rights to access health records of deceased patients if the health record was created after 1st November 1991.

As with all other forms of access to health records, there are exemptions to the right to access the health record of a deceased patient. These are:

- where there is reasonable belief that accessing the health record or a specific part of it would cause you, or somebody else, serious physical or mental harm to the person requesting access.
- where information about a third person would be disclosed.
- if the patient made a request that their health record or information in it is not disclosed to a specific person and it is that person making the request.

Where a person is granted access to their deceased relatives health record, they may find that they are not given access to the complete record, for one of the reasons above.

⚥ Visiting patients

You may wonder why we have left the issue of visitors until this chapter. It is because although visitors may be welcomed by patients, by visiting a patient a visitor can have access to the patient's confidential information and information about the patient's healthcare needs and treatment that the visitor would otherwise not have access to.

One aspect of accepting treatment is being able to see family and friends whilst receiving that treatment, and visitors are generally encouraged to see patients in hospital and other care settings because it is recognised that this usually has a positive effect on the patient.

However, you will probably find that most clinical areas have set visiting times when visitors are allowed to visit and at other times specific permission is needed to enter the clinical area. The reason for the restriction is to ensure that patients, not just your relative but all patients, have an opportunity to be uninterrupted. This is also to allow time for patients to have their tests and investigations undertaken and for them to be able to see their healthcare team in private.

Hospitals and other care environments are private places and so they can control who is allowed into the property. This means that they can restrict entry, as with visiting times, or prevent it altogether if it was felt that a particular visitor was causing harm to a patient by their presence.

If you need to visit a patient outside of the set visiting times you will need to speak to one of the healthcare practitioners working in that clinical area and explain why you are unable to visit during the normal visiting times and ask permission to do so. Most clinical areas try to be accommodating but are mindful of the need for patients to rest and recuperate and also that certain times are particularly busy. However, it is likely that you will be allowed to visit for a set time, which may be much shorter than normal visiting hours, that is convenient to you but does not cause too much disturbance to other patients or to the routine of the clinical area.

Patients can also request that a particular relative or friend is not allowed to visit them. Obviously, it would be useful if the patient discussed this with the person considered but if this is not possible the staff can enforce this on the patient's behalf.

Visitors can also be asked to leave a clinical area after they have been granted entry if they are being disruptive or causing distress to their relative or another patient. This is also the case if the relative is accompanying a patient to a hospital appointment.

Child patients and child visitors

Where the patient is a child, particularly a younger child, there is usually a more relaxed approach to visiting by relatives, although visiting may be restricted to parents and immediate family members. However, a parent who causes distress to their child may find that they either have their visiting time limited or are not allowed to visit, in the best interests of the child. This would be a last resort and would need legal opinion so as not to interfere with the parent's right to respect for family life, which includes the right to regular contact between family members.

When the visitor is a child, you may find that it is recommended that those below a certain age do not visit you. This is for two reasons. The first is to protect the child from picking up an infection or other illness due to their immune system being less mature than an adult's, particularly babies or very young children. Secondly, children can find the clinical environment scary if they are not fully prepared for what they could see. Many clinical areas are very busy and noisy and there are very sick individuals who may look strange to the child, and some of these patients may experience an emergency during the visiting time.

If you want to have a child visit you whilst you are in hospital, it is best to discuss this with your healthcare practitioner as they may be able to suggest a more suitable time or even arrange for you to have your visit in a less clinical looking part of the ward.

You also need to consider the effect of a young child visiting you on the other patients. A child who becomes frightened or anxious may disturb the other patients through their reactions, for instance a very young child who is running about or cries uncontrollably.

CHAPTER 7

DECISION-MAKING AROUND
THE END OF LIFE

Chapter 7 deals with some difficult issues centred around patient rights in relation to dying and death. We have approached the chapter so that issues that arise before death are discussed first, then the issues around death and dying itself, and finally those issues that occur after the death of a patient.

The issues we discuss in this chapter are resuscitation and do not attempt resuscitation orders, withholding and withdrawal of treatment, followed by suicide and euthanasia. We then move on to consider the definition of death, how death is certified and registering a death.

The chapter ends by examining organ donation.

Resuscitation/Do not attempt resuscitation recommendation

Resuscitation, or cardio-pulmonary resuscitation to give it its full title, is often seen in television dramas where it is referred to as CPR and terms such as *the patient has crashed,* or *the crash cart* are used. It is often portrayed as being highly successful, so long as the hero doctor or nurse is involved in the *crash team.*

Excuse our cynicism, but whilst there is a very high success rate in achieving a survival, what is not reflected in television programmes is that patients who survive resuscitation do not in fact tend to survive for long. The NHS website suggests that overall success is between 10 and 20%. Even where a patient is successfully resuscitated, they can suffer a range of injuries ranging from bruising to fractures, particularly of the ribs, through to organ damage, such as puncturing of the lungs, to brain damage.

It is because of the low success rate and the devastating affect it can have on a patient, as well as the emotional distress that can be caused for both patients and their families, that discussing whether resuscitation should be attempted at the latter stages of a patient's illness has become more commonplace.

These discussions can result in what is termed a *do not attempt resuscitation recommendation* usually abbreviated to DNACPR, or sometimes DNAR. Do not attempt resuscitation recommendations have recently been termed *do not attempt resuscitation orders* or *do not attempt resuscitation notices*. The change in terminology from being a *notice* or an *order* to a *recommendation* is intended to reflect that circumstances can change and that a DNACPR is intended to assist a decision as to whether to implement resuscitation on a specific patient at a specific point in time. A DNACPR is a decision that needs to be made on a clinical assessment based on the patient's best interests. It is important to note here the discussion on best interests in chapter 5 *When the patient lacks the capacity to consent for their own healthcare needs,* where it was noted that it can never be in a patient's best interests to receive treatment that they have previously refused when competent to make their own treatment decisions.

A DNACPR is a decision made by the healthcare team of a patient that cardio-pulmonary resuscitation would not be in the patient's best interests in stated circumstances because it would be futile, (i.e., not successful). The decision is made at a time when it is possible to take all considerations into account in advance of the time when the patient may need resuscitation. Essentially, a DNACPR can be likened to the advance decision that was discussed in chapter 5 that a patient can make to refuse treatment in the anticipation of being unable to make a decision in the future. The difference is that a DNACPR is not made by the patient but by members of the healthcare team caring for and treating the patient.

Because a DNACPR is based on a patient's condition at the time the decision is made and is made in anticipation of a future event, it is possible that the patient's condition will improve to such an extent that the healthcare practitioner who would consider resuscitation at the time the patient needs it, would decide to initiate resuscitation. It is possible for the healthcare practitioner to do this because a DNACPR is not legally binding. Rather, a DNACPR is an additional piece of information that can be taken into account when considering a patient's best interests to decide upon what treatment to give to a patient or not to give.

Legal validity of a do not attempt resuscitation recommendation

Although a DNACPR is not legally binding, they are legally valid. By this we mean that although a DNACPR may be in place for a particular patient, the healthcare practitioner may make a decision whilst the patient is in need of resuscitation that it is in the patient's best interests for resuscitation to be implemented. Thus, there is no obligation on that healthcare practitioner to abide by the recommendation in the DNACPR. However, if the healthcare practitioner had decided to accept the recommendation in the DNACPR and not initiate resuscitation, this would be a legally valid decision and the healthcare practitioner would not be failing in their duty to the patient.

To be legally valid, there are several principles which need to be followed when a DNACPR is made. These principles were reiterated in the legal case of R (on the application of Tracey) v

Cambridge University Hospitals NHS Trust [2014] which had to consider whether a DNACPR was appropriately used for a particular patient (Mrs Tracey).

The principles are that:

- The patient should be involved in discussions whenever it is possible to do so
- If the patient does not wish to be involved or is unable to be involved, their relatives should be invited to be part of the discussion
- Any decision should be made in the patient's best interests
- The decision to make a DNACPR should be communicated to the patient, or to their attorney if they have a lasting power or attorney, or to their relatives if it would cause distress to the patient
- The healthcare team does not need the consent of the patient to make a DNACPR, because they cannot lawfully give treatment that they consider to be clinically futile
- If the patient disagrees with the decision to make a DNACPR, they can ask for a review of the decision via a second opinion. If the patient is unaware of the DNACPR, the patient's attorney, or failing this their relatives, may request the second opinion. However, the request for a second option does not have to be granted if the original decision was made after a thorough discussion by the healthcare team.
- The DNACPR decision needs to be recorded in the patient's healthcare notes, and most healthcare organisations have a specific form for this purpose
- A DNACPR cannot be made for a number of patients at the same time; they are for specific patients, made after a discussion about that patient
- There should be a policy in place within the healthcare organisation which outlines the use of DNACPRs

- As a DNACPR is an advance decision that it would be futile for the patient to receive cardio-pulmonary resuscitation, all healthcare practitioners have to follow it unless they can demonstrate that circumstances have changed since the DNACPR decision was made and cardio-pulmonary resuscitation would no longer be contrary to the patient's best interests or futile.

A DNACPR can be written to last a defined period of time, or it can last until it is either used or is no longer needed. A DNACPR can be reviewed if the patient's condition changes, or it can be removed from the patient's healthcare record altogether. Any changes to a DNACPR, including its removal, should be communicated to the patient, their attorney if they have a lasting power of attorney, or to their relatives.

Patient refusal of resuscitation

If a patient does not want to receive cardio-pulmonary resuscitation, rather than relying upon a DNACPR they can either make an advance decision that covers resuscitation or make a Lasting Power of Attorney (LPA) and inform their attorney of this (both advance decisions and LPAs are discussed in chapter 5 *When the patient lacks the capacity to consent for their own healthcare needs*).

Withholding and withdrawal of treatment

In chapter 4 *Refusing treatment*, we saw that an adult patient who is competent to make their own treatment decisions can legally refuse a specific treatment, or indeed all treatment, even if this refusal will mean that the patient suffers harm or would die as a result of not having the treatment. We also saw that if a patient had given their consent to receive a specific treatment and then changed their mind after the treatment had commenced, they could withdraw the consent they had given, and the treatment should be stopped as soon as it was safe to do so.

Refusal to give consent and withdrawing of their consent by a competent adult patient is one way that treatment can be withheld or withdrawn. This section considers how treatment can lawfully be withheld or withdrawn by healthcare practitioners.

Withholding treatment

Healthcare practitioners can lawfully withhold treatment based on the clinical needs of the patient. When considering healthcare decision-making in chapter 2 *Engaging with healthcare*, it was noted that healthcare practitioners can only legally offer you treatment that they believe is clinically appropriate to meet your specific healthcare needs. Therefore, if a healthcare practitioner does not believe that a specific treatment will meet your healthcare needs, they do not have to offer that treatment to you. By not offering you a specific treatment, the healthcare practitioner is effectively withholding that treatment from you, based on your healthcare needs.

If the patient is not able to consent for themselves, the healthcare practitioner is only able to give treatment based on the patient's best interests. Best interests was explored in chapter 5 *When the patient lacks the capacity to consent for their own healthcare needs*. There it was stated that the term best interests is a form of shorthand to mean 'what decision on treatment would be best for this particular patient'. If the healthcare practitioner does not believe that a particular treatment is best for the patient based on the patient's healthcare needs, they do not have to provide it and thus will withhold it from the patient.

Withdrawing treatment

Withdrawing treatment is different from withholding treatment. A decision has already been made at some point previously that the treatment the healthcare practitioner is intending to withdraw was considered to be clinically appropriate to offer to a competent patient, or in the best interests of a patient who lacked the capacity to make their own treatment decision.

Treatment withdrawal is generally considered near the end of a patient's life when the treatment is not providing a useful benefit to the patient and may even be causing harm to the patient.

Legal basis for withdrawing treatment

The significant case in relation to withdrawal of treatment is Airedale NHS Trust v Bland [1993]. The case concerned Anthony 'Tony' Bland who was 21 years old at the time of the case and had been in a persistent vegetative state for over 3 years, having been injured in the Hillsborough disaster. The case was brought to determine if the treatment that Mr Bland was receiving, artificial feeding through a tube through the nose into the stomach and antibiotics treatment for infections, could be withdrawn.

It was recognised that withdrawing the artificial feeding would result in Mr Bland's death. Both the healthcare practitioners treating Mr Bland and his family supported withdrawing the treatment. The hospital where Mr Bland was being treated asked the court for a declaration as to the lawfulness of withdrawing the treatment.

It was noted in the case that

> 'the unanimous opinion of all the doctors who had examined him was that there was no hope whatsoever of recovery or improvement of any kind in his condition and that there was no reasonable possibility of his ever emerging to a cognitive

sapient state from his existing persistent vegetative state in which, although he continued to breathe unaided and his digestion continued to function, he could not see, hear, taste, smell or communicate in any way, was incapable of involuntary movement, could not feel pain and had no cognitive function' (Airedale NHS Trust v Bland [1993] at page 821).

The court had to decide if withdrawing the treatment would mean that the healthcare practitioners had failed in their duty of care to Mr Bland, and because Mr Bland was unable to participate in treatment decisions, what Mr Bland's best interests were.

Where withdrawing treatment will lead to the death of the patient, it can be said that it will always be in the patient's best interests to receive the treatment so that they could continue to live. However, in the case Lord Goff said that the question about a patient's best interests should not be framed to ask '

whether it is in the best interests of the patient that he should die. The question is whether it is in the best interests of the patient that his life should be prolonged by the continuance of this form of medical treatment or care' (Airedale NHS Trust v Bland [1993] at page 869).

Considering whether it is in the best interests of a patient to receive treatment that will not improve their condition, Lord Goff stated

'I cannot see that medical treatment is appropriate or requisite simply to prolong a patient's life when such treatment has no therapeutic purpose of any kind, as where it is futile because the patient is unconscious and there is no prospect of any improvement in his condition' (Airedale NHS Trust v Bland [1993] at page 870).

When discussing if treatment has a benefit for the patient, Lord Keith stated that decisions regarding whether a particular treatment has a benefit for the patient, that is, whether it is in the patient's best interests to receive it, are ones that should be left to the healthcare practitioners who are treating the patient.

In the case, it was held that Mr Bland had no prospect of recovery, and it was not in his best interests to receive treatment that was clinically futile. Also, that as Mr Bland had never given his consent to the treatment, the healthcare practitioners would not be breaching their duty of care to him to withdraw treatment that they did not consider to be in his best interests.

As a result of the outcome of the Bland case, it is lawful for healthcare practitioners to withdraw treatment from patients, even if this will result in the patient's death, if it is not in the patient's best interests to continue to receive the treatment because one or more of the following applies:

- the patient will never recover
- the burden of receiving the treatment outweighs any benefit from it
- the treatment is futile

One final point to make about treatment withdrawal. In legal terms, it is not the withdrawal of the treatment that is the cause of the patient's death. It is the patient's underlying condition that is the cause of the patient's death. This is because the treatment that is being withdrawn is only prolonging the inevitable consequence of the patient's condition.

Suicide

Whilst it may seem strange to be discussing suicide in a book on healthcare rights, some patients find that they want to end their life at a time of their choosing and there can be a lot of confusion around suicide and what is and is not legal.

At one time it was a criminal offence to *attempt* to commit, or to commit, suicide in England, Northern Ireland, and Wales, but never Scotland. However, since the introduction of the Suicide Act 1961 this is no longer the case, and a person may commit suicide or attempt suicide without committing a criminal offence (it was the Criminal Justice Act (Northern Ireland) 1966 that decriminalised suicide and attempted suicide in Northern Ireland).

A word here about terminology. Within legislation, such as the Suicide Act 1961, the term 'commit suicide' is used. However, it is now recognised that this term has negative inferences linked with the previous illegality of suicide. Likewise, terms such as 'completed suicide', 'successful suicide' or 'failed suicide attempt' are problematic because positive connotations are attached to suicide, and negative connotations are attached to a suicide attempt resulting in non-fatal injuries. The Support After Suicide Partnership, a charity that works to support those affected by suicide, suggests that the terms 'took their life', 'died by/from suicide' and 'ended their own life' are more suitable. Where we have used the term 'commit suicide' here, it is used because it is within the legislation, but we fully recognise how problematic the term is and have used alternatives where possible.

Assisted suicide

Some patients are physically unable to end their own life entirely unaided, or do not know how to do so, and require the help of someone else to assist them. Although the Suicide Act 1961 removed the criminal offence of committing, or attempting to commit, suicide it did not do the same for assisting suicide.

In relation to assisted suicide, section 2[1] of the Suicide Act 1961 originally stated that *'a person who aids, abets, counsels or procures the suicide of another, or an attempt by another*

*to commit suicide, shall be liable on conviction on indictment
to imprisonment for a term not exceeding fourteen years.'*

It can be seen that the offence of assisting suicide is quite
broad and can be just giving information or advice to someone.

Because Scotland never had a criminal offence of suicide, the
law on assisting suicide does not apply to Scotland, although
if someone were to assist another person in their suicide in
Scotland, they could be prosecuted for offences such as reckless
endangerment or culpable homicide.

A number of challenges to the law of assisted suicide have
been brought over the years, including through Parliament and
the courts. As a result of these, a number of changes to the law
on assisted suicide have occurred. The Suicide Act 1961 was
amended by the Coroners and Justice Act 2009 so that section
2[1] now states:

A person ('D') commits an offence if —

*(a) D does an act capable of encouraging or assisting the
suicide or attempted suicide of another person, and*

*(b) D's act was intended to encourage or assist suicide or
an attempt at suicide*

Whilst section 2[4] has added that

*'no proceedings shall be instituted for an offence under this
section except by or with the consent of the Director of Public
Prosecutions'.*

This means that although assisting suicide is a criminal offence,
it will not always be prosecuted and requires the approval of
the Director of Public Prosecutions. In September 2009, the
Director of Public Prosecutions issued the guidance on which a
decision on whether to prosecute someone for assisted suicide
would be made (Crown Prosecution Service 2014).

The guidance has a number of factors that would favour prosecution, and a number that favour not prosecuting. Those that favour prosecution include:

- The person who committed suicide (known as the victim) being under 18
- The victim not having the capacity to make a decision
- No prior communication of a desire to end their life by the victim
- The person who assisted the suicide (known as the suspect) pressuring the victim
- The suspect gaining financially by the victim's death
- The suspect having assisted a number of victims
- If the suspect is a healthcare practitioner
- The suspect not reporting their assistance to the police

The reasons not to prosecute are based around the victim making a voluntary decision to end their own life, the suspect only assisted them out of compassion, the assistance of the suspect was minimal, they tried to dissuade the victim but were unable to do so, and the suspect reported their assistance to the police.

As can be seen, everything else being equal, a healthcare practitioner is more likely to be prosecuted for assisting suicide than if the assistance came from a friend or relative.

On conviction, a person may still receive up to 14 years imprisonment for assisting another person with their suicide.

Euthanasia

A translation of euthanasia is *good death*, although since the 1930s the term has come to mean when one person ends the life of another at the first person's request because their pain or suffering is too much, and they want to end their life. As well as euthanasia, there are many different terms in use. These include mercy killing, passive euthanasia, active euthanasia, assisted dying, and termination of life. Whatever term is employed, it is used to describe the intentional taking of a life at the request of the person who will die. You may sometime see the terms 'voluntary' or 'involuntary' added to any of the terms in use, however, this is a misnomer as ending the life of someone who does not want their own death is homicide.

Another term in use that causes an issue is that of 'physician assisted suicide'. There is a difference between euthanasia and assisted suicide, so the term is inappropriate for that reason alone. However, as we have just seen in the previous section, a healthcare practitioner who assists a patient with their suicide is more likely to be prosecuted than if the assistance had been given by a relative.

The difference between assisted suicide and euthanasia is that in assisted suicide, the person who is ending their own life is able to undertake at least part of the act that results in death. They require assistance but are not totally reliant upon the assistant. In euthanasia, the person who wishes to die is unable to perform the act that will result in their death. Euthanasia requires someone to perform an act that will result in another person's' death.

It can be seen that euthanasia is a step on from assisting someone in their own death. It is because euthanasia requires a person to actively end the life of another person, even at that person's request, that euthanasia is illegal in many countries. Euthanasia is illegal in more countries than it is legal. Some of the countries where euthanasia is currently legal include:

- Belgium
- Canada
- Colombia
- Luxembourg

- Netherlands
- New Zealand
- Spain
- Switzerland
- In addition, some states within the United States of America and some states in Australia

Although the above countries have legalised euthanasia, they have done so to a greater or lesser extent, and some require very strict criteria to be satisfied before euthanasia can be caried out.

In the United Kingdom, euthanasia is currently illegal. As the law presently stands, if one person intentionally takes the life of another person, even at that person's request, the person undertaking the act could be charged with murder or manslaughter. There have been various petitions and calls for euthanasia to be made legal in the United Kingdom, including attempts to introduce law in Parliament. So far, these have not been successful.

Because euthanasia is illegal in the United Kingdom, some patients who wish to end their life but are unable to do so themselves and wish to protect their relatives and friends from fear of prosecution decide to travel to a country where euthanasia is legal, and have their life ended in that country. Some countries do not allow what is euphemistically called 'death tourism', travelling from one country to another for the express reason to die in the country travelled to, and have a residency criterion before someone can undergo euthanasia.

If a patient, who is unable to perform the act that will end their own life, travels to another country to die, they will inevitably need the assistance of others to travel to that country. Those who assist the patient to travel to another country to die could find that on their return they face the prospect of being prosecuted for assisting suicide. Any decision to prosecute someone would be based on the guidance on assisted suicide discussed in the previous section.

Definition of death

There are two types of death: medical death and legal death. Medical death comes before legal death because someone has to be declared medically dead before legal death comes into effect. Legal death is the recognition that a person is no longer alive, so that they no longer have a legal identity and their documentation such as a passport or driving licence becomes invalid, and their body may be lawfully disposed of, for instance by being buried or cremated. Also, on legal death a person is no longer capable of owning possessions and their will may be enacted.

It seems relatively easy to determine if someone is dead or not. Yet in reality, this has not always been the case. Death used to be based on someone ceasing breathing and not having a beating heart. So, when the person's breathing stopped and their heart stopped, they were seen as being dead.

Brainstem death

The issue with the definition of death being based on breathing and heart activity stopping is that with modern resuscitation techniques it is possible to successfully revive someone who is technically dead. Also, when a patient has open heart surgery their lungs and heart will be stopped and the patient will be kept alive through the use of a by-pass machine, as in it bypasses the lungs and heart and directly provides oxygen to the body. At the end of the operation the patient's heart is restarted and the lungs work again. But if the lungs and heart have stopped, is the patient dead or alive during the operation?

A similar situation occurs with patients in intensive care units who receive artificial ventilation via machines to keep them alive.

The line between life and death starts to become blurred and so another method of determining if a person is alive or dead is needed. In 1968, brainstem death was introduced as a way of determining if a person has died in the United States. It was accepted as a means of determining death in the United Kingdom in 1976.

The brainstem sits between the brain and the spinal cord. Most bodily reflexes pass through the brainstem, including breathing and heart beating. Brainstem death refers to the situation where the reflexes that pass through the spinal cord are absent. The patient is unconscious, although they may appear as if they are merely sleeping. Their ability to breathe is lost and they are only alive because their breathing is being supported by machines. If the machines are stopped the patient will not regain consciousness or breathe on their own.

To determine that a patient is brainstem dead, a very strict set of criteria have to be met. These include that the patient is unable to breathe unaided and that certain reflexes can be demonstrated to be absent. If a patient is declared to be brainstem dead, the machinery that is providing their artificial ventilation etc. can be removed. Because of the seriousness of a declaration that someone is brainstem dead, it has to be undertaken by two doctors and the tests have to be repeated. The patient would be declared dead if the results are negative on the completion of the second set of tests.

Legal definition of death

It may seem bizarre, but there is no statutory definition of death in the United Kingdom. There is no Act of Parliament that provides a definition of death. Neither has the common law, through legal cases, provided a definition of death.

The legal position on defining death is to accept the medical definition of death. There are thus two ways of legally and medically determining if a person is dead in the United Kingdom, these being absence of cardiopulmonary function (no heartbeat and no breathing), which is the test which will be used for the vast majority of people, and brainstem death.

Certifying death

In order to start the legal process of recognising the death of a person, that person first needs to be declared medically dead as noted in the last section. Once the person has been declared to be dead, a certificate is issued which confirms that the person has died and the cause of their death. The official title for this certificate is a 'medical certificate of cause of death'.

In chapter 2 *Engaging with healthcare*, it was noted that some areas of healthcare practice are restricted as to which healthcare practitioners can undertake them. The certification of death is a restricted activity and is regulated by the Births and Deaths Registration Act 1953, which only permits registered medical practitioners, that is doctors, to issues a medical certificate of cause of death.

Normally a medical certificate of cause of death will be issued by the doctor who attended to the patient during their last illness. There is no definition of who this is, but it should be someone who cared for the patient during their last illness and is aware of the patient's medical history and is able to access the patient's healthcare records if necessary. Those who have responsibility for ensuring that a medical certificate of cause of death is issued will be a hospital consultant in charge of the patient's care if the patient died in hospital, or the patient's general practitioner.

If the patient was not seen by a doctor in the 28 days preceding their death or the cause of death cannot be determined, the death can be referred to a coroner.

🔲 Verification of death

Although only a doctor can *certify* that a patient has died, other healthcare practitioners can *verify* that a patient has died. Verification is different to certifying the death of a patient. Certifying a patient's death results in the issuing of a certificate which includes the date and cause of death, that can be used for legal purposes. Verification of death simply means that the healthcare practitioner confirms that the patient has in fact died.

Healthcare practitioners need to ensure that their employer allows them to verify death before they undertake this role. There are no specific requirements other than being allowed to do so by their employer. In reality, most employers require that healthcare practitioners undertake a period of training and are assessed as being competent in the role before they undertake it.

Registering a death and the role of the coroner

Once a patient's relative has medical certification of cause of death they can start the process of legally registering the death of the patient. If it is not possible for a doctor to issue a medical certificate of cause of death, or a post-mortem or inquest into the patient's death is needed, the death will be reported to a coroner.

A coroner is a form of judge whose role is to investigate the cause of death, although they have other roles too which are outside the area of our discussion, such as investigating treasure trove (this is basically treasure that is hidden until found by someone).

Coroners will become involved if a patient's death is suspicious; the cause of death is unknown; the death was unnatural or the result of violence; the patient took their own life, died from an accident or industrial disease; or the patient's death was as a result of negligence. Coroners are subject to the rules of the Coroners and Justice Act 2009, and according to section 5 of the Act the coroner's role is to determine '*who the deceased was*', and '*how, when and where the deceased came by his or her death*'.

Where the coroner is able to determine the cause of death, they can issue a certificate which allows the death to be registered with the Registrar of Births, Deaths and Marriages. If the coroner is not able to state the cause of death, they can arrange for a post-mortem to be undertaken to determine the cause of death. There is no right to object to a post-mortem that is ordered by a coroner.

If the post-mortem reveals the cause of death, the coroner will notify the Registrar of Births, Deaths and Marriages what the cause of death is, so that the death can be registered. If the cause of death is as a result of unnatural causes or violence, or the death occurs in prison or in police custody, the coroner is required to hold an inquest into the person's death.

Normally a medical certificate of cause of death is required to register a death before a funeral can be held. If the coroner needs to hold an inquest, it would not normally be possible to register the death. However, a coroner is able to issue an interim death certificate for the purpose of holding a funeral where the cause of death is not in dispute.

ϰ Next steps after a person has died

There are several websites, both by the government and voluntary organisations, which provide guidance on what to do after the death of a relative. The key point is to register the death of the patient with the Registrar of Births, Deaths and Marriages within 5 days (in Scotland this is extended to 8 days). Not registering a death is a criminal offence.

To register a death, as well as the medical certificate of cause of death, the person registering the death will also need to take the following documents with them to the register office:

- Birth certificate
- Marriage or civil partnership certificate
- Driving licence and passport
- Proof of address, such as a utility bill
- NHS card
- Council tax bill
- National insurance number of both the deceased and their surviving spouse or civil partner

If any of these are not available, it is still possible to register the patient's death so long as the person registering the death knows:

- the full name of the person who died, including any previous names they used
- their last address
- their date and place of birth
- their occupation, or if they are retired their last occupation
- details of their state pension or other state benefits they were receiving
- the details of their spouse or civil partner

Once the death has been registered a certificate for the registration of death (often known as a death certificate) and a certificate for burial and cremation will be issued by the register office. The certificate for burial and cremation is needed before a funeral can take place as it is illegal to dispose of a body without the certificate, which has to be given to the funeral director or crematorium. Anyone can arrange a person's funeral and there is no minimum or maximum time limit within which a funeral has to take place.

The reason for the issuing of the certificate for the registration of death is that it allows the deceased person's affairs to be managed.

Various government departments need to be informed of the person's death, but this can only be done after the death has been registered. There is a government website called 'TellUsOnce' which has information and links for this, and this is in the resources section at the end of the book.

Organ Donation

The reason for including a discussion on organ donation is that it is related to the rights of patients, their relatives and their carers in two key ways. The first is in relation to the consent for donation, and the second relates to the rights of relatives.

Consent for organ donation

The law in relation to consent for the donation of organs after death is different to the ethical and legal principles of consent as we have discussed it so far in this book, and in fact turns most of what has been said on its head (with one exception).

The United Kingdom used to have what was termed an 'opt in' system of organ donation. This meant that someone had to opt into the system by registering their desire to have their organs donated after their death. They were also advised to discuss their decision with their relatives, for reasons which will become clear in the next section. So far, this is in keeping with consent as we have discussed it; a patient is asked to give their consent for something to happen.

What has changed is that England, Scotland and Wales have moved to an 'opt out' system of consent for organ donation. The exception, which was referred to above, is Northern Ireland which has retained the opt in system.

In an opt out system, instead of permission being requested

from someone for their organs to be used after their death, as would be expected using the principles of consent we have so far discussed, in relation to organ donation there is a presumption of consent unless the person has specifically registered their wish to opt out of donating their organs.

Wales was the first country of the United Kingdom to move to an opt out system in December 2015 and uses the term 'deemed consent'.

England was next on 20th May 2020 and uses the term 'presumed consent'.

Scotland stared using an opt out system on 26th March 2021 and uses the term 'deemed authorisation'.

Deemed consent, presumed consent and deemed authorisation all mean the same thing, which is that unless someone specifically registers their decision not to have their organs donated after their death, it will be presumed that they have consented for this to happen.

The presumption of consent for organ donation does not apply to those:

- under 18
- who have opted out
- in excluded groups

Those in excluded groups include individuals:

- who do not have the capacity to be able to make a decision about organ donation
- who are living temporarily in the country where it operates
- who have lived in one of the three countries for less than 12 months before their death
- who are visiting the country

It is important to note that an opt out system of consent, or the presumption of consent, can only be used for organ donation and not for any other form of treatment.

ℛ Relatives and organ donation

Strictly speaking, the use of presumed consent for organ donation means that the deceased person's organs can be used without seeking permission from anyone else unless they have opted out. However, England, Scotland and Wales all use what is termed a 'soft presumed consent' approach. This means that it is presumed that the person has consented, but their relatives are allowed to have a veto. The reason for this is that it allows those individuals who object to having their organs removed after their death, but who have not formally registered their objection, to have their wishes respected.

In chapter 2 *Engaging with healthcare*, the role of relatives in a patient's healthcare was discussed. It was noted that there were two exceptions to the general principle that relatives do not have a say in a patient's healthcare. The first exception was in relation to mental health legislation where the concept of the 'nearest relative' is used. The second exception is in relation to organ donation.

A relative is able to be involved in two ways. If the deceased patient has not registered their objection to organ donation before their death, the relative is able to put forward the patient's known wishes and to veto the use of the patient's organs according to these wishes. Secondly, if the patient is in one of the excluded groups, then presumed consent will not apply, but the relative is able to state whether the patient would have wanted their organs used for donation or not.

It is important that people discuss organ donation with their loved ones. The NHS organ donation website allows people to opt out of organ donation, as well as enabling people to register their wish to be an organ doner. It is possible to choose specifically which organs you do and do not wish to donate should you die. There is also support in how to manage these difficult conversations with loved ones, so that in the event of your death they are aware of the decisions you have made. This can be very helpful in preventing loved ones having to make decisions on your behalf, and ensures your wishes are followed.

Not all relatives are able to exercise their right to be involved. Similar to the 'nearest relative', organ donation legislation has a hierarchical list of relatives who may provide consent for a patient's organ(s) to be donated and used in transplantation, or to refuse to give consent, after their death. In the legislation, this hierarchical list is known as the list of 'individuals in a qualifying relationship', hence the term that is used to describe them.

This hierarchy is contained in section 27(4) of the Human Tissue Act 2004 and is:

1. *spouse, civil partner or partner*
2. *parent or child*
3. *brother or sister*
4. *grandparent or grandchild*
5. *child of a person falling within (c)*
6. *stepfather or stepmother*
7. *half-brother or half-sister*
8. *friend of longstanding*

As with the 'nearest relative', it is the person highest in the list who would be expected to take on the role.

CHAPTER 8

QUESTIONING HEALTHCARE

When we were originally planning the book, this chapter was called 'if something goes wrong' or 'when things go wrong'. However, we realised that it is much more complicated than having a chapter that deals with healthcare mistakes and errors and the rights of the patient when this occurs. This is because despite appearances, there are times when nothing has in fact gone wrong, but it still doesn't *feel* right. Alternatively, there are times when care or treatment does not go as planned but does not result in a poor outcome for the patient.

We realised that the important point is to ask questions about healthcare in general, and in particular about the healthcare you, and those you care for, receive and about the healthcare practitioners who provide the care and treatment for you. When there is a perception that things are wrong, or may be going wrong, or if they have already gone wrong, it is important to question it. Therefore, this is what this chapter is about; how to question healthcare.

This chapter discusses the various aspects and ways of questioning healthcare. This includes how to raise your concerns when things go wrong, or you believe they have gone wrong or when things are not as you would want them. As well as raising concerns, the chapter considers whether you can expect someone to say sorry if a mistake has occurred as well as honesty and transparency from healthcare providers through the duty of candour and a healthcare practitioner's professional duty of candour.

Chapter 8 then moves on to consider complaints and how a complaint can be made, before analysing negligence, including what it is and how it is decided. The chapter ends by discussing the standard to which healthcare practitioners are held and how to report a concern about a particular healthcare practitioner to their regulatory body.

Raising concerns

When discussing decision-making for your healthcare needs in chapter 2 *Engaging with healthcare*, we noted that as part of your role as a patient you need to inform your healthcare practitioner(s) if you do not have all the information you need to make a decision. We also discussed the situation where you may want a different treatment to the one that is being offered to you, and how you can ask for a second opinion if you are unsure about an aspect of your care and treatment.

All of these are forms of raising a concern as they inform the healthcare practitioner that you have a query about your care and treatment that you would like to be addressed. A concern does not have to be a major issue that has arisen. It can be, as in the examples given, something that needs to be clarified or addressed so that you can decide upon what is best to meet your healthcare needs.

However, there are occasions when you have more than a query or question that needs to be addressed, or when you believe that something is going wrong or has already gone wrong. It does not necessarily have to relate to your healthcare but can be about the care or treatment you witness another patient receiving or the manner and attitude of a healthcare practitioner.

Although we discuss the patient as the one who should raise a concern in the rest of this section, concerns can be raised by anyone including relatives and carers. If you have a concern about something that is happening, a first step would be to raise this with your healthcare practitioner. In many instances they will be able to deal with your concern and rectify it. Even if the healthcare practitioner is not able to deal with your concern themselves, they will know who they should approach to report it so that it can be addressed.

If you have a concern about poor practice that you have witnessed or are witnessing, you need to raise it with an appropriate person. It may be that you cannot, or do not feel able to, raise it with the healthcare practitioner(s) involved. Most healthcare practitioners work within a management structure and so raising your concern with the healthcare practitioner's line manager is a logical step to take.

Raising a concern is not easy as you are effectively telling someone that something has gone wrong or is in danger of going wrong and this is not always easy to hear. However, it is your right to raise a concern and healthcare practitioners have to act for the benefit of their patients. If something is not going as planned, they need to be aware of it so that they can address the issue.

By raising a concern, you are not being a 'troublemaker'. It may be that no-one has realised that the issue is causing a problem and it is only by you raising a concern that it is drawn to their attention. If the issue is already known about and in the process of being addressed, then you raising it is not problematic because the healthcare practitioner simply needs to explain that the issue is being addressed.

If you are ever in doubt as to whether to raise a concern, ask yourself what could happen if the issue were to continue. Generally, the earlier a concern is raised, the easier it is to deal with before it becomes a major issue.

If you do need to raise a concern, you should do so as soon as possible. This will help prevent the issue from escalating and also mean that the details are not forgotten. You should be as factual as possible and state why you are raising the concern, what your concern is and, if relevant, what outcome you would like to see happen. We would recommend that, if possible, you keep a record of your concerns, who you raised it with and the date and time you raised it.

If a matter you have raised has not been addressed to your satisfaction you may have to escalate your concern and the next step may be to make a complaint. Making a complaint is dealt with below.

Healthcare practitioners and raising a concern

It isn't just patients who should report a concern if they have one. Healthcare practitioners have a professional duty to raise any concerns they have about their colleagues or the systems and processes they work within. Examples include raising concerns about:

- Staff levels – where the healthcare practitioner considers the staffing in a clinical area to be unsafe.
- A colleague whose practice is thought to be below the required standard
- Equipment that is still being used, despite malfunctioning and a request being made for its repair
- Colleagues who are acting unprofessionally toward their patients

Healthcare practitioners are also expected to challenge any instances of poor practice they witness patients receiving.

◨ Raising a concern and whistleblowing

Whistleblowing is a particular way of raising a concern. It usually happens because an individual has had no success in having an issue addressed internally and they need to raise their concern externally to their organisation for it to be addressed. It is also possible to whistle blow within an organisation.

Legal protection exists for whistle-blowers so that they do not suffer as a result of raising a concern by 'blowing the whistle' on an issue that is happening within their organisation. This protection is through the provision in the Public Interest Disclosure Act 1998.

In order to qualify for the protection under the Public Interest Disclosure Act 1998, the person making the disclosure (that is, the person raising their concern) has to meet certain criteria which are set out in the Act. These include the reason for making the disclosure, and that the disclosure has to be made to an appropriate person or organisation. One of the accepted reasons to make a disclosure is to protect the health and safety of individuals. 'Appropriate person or organisation' includes employers, legal advisers and individuals or organisations that are able to act upon the information. In healthcare, this would include the healthcare practitioner, regulatory bodies, and organisations that have regulatory oversight of healthcare such as the Care Quality Commission (CQC).

A person should only 'whistle blow' after they have exhausted the internal mechanism for raising a concern within their organisation or where they reasonably believe that their concern is not being addressed.

Apologies and saying sorry

Sometimes as a patient you do not want to make a complaint or to bring a legal or regulatory case against someone. All you want is for someone to acknowledge that something did not go quite as it should and to say sorry. However, there is still a mistaken belief amongst healthcare practitioners that they should not apologise or say sorry to a patient for something that happens to them.

The reasoning behind this belief is that if a healthcare practitioner were to say sorry, they are admitting that whatever they are apologising for was their fault, and they are now liable for that event. Essentially, there is a belief that it will cause problems for them!

Thankfully not all healthcare practitioners think this way, because it is totally wrong. Before we go into why it is wrong, let's look at what an apology is. We are aware that we all know what an apology is, but healthcare law has a specific definition of an apology. That definition is, according to Regulation 20(7) of The Health and Social Care Act 2008 (Regulated Activities) Regulations 2014, '*an expression of sorrow or regret in respect of a notifiable safety incident*'. That is the legal definition, but an apology can be as simple as a healthcare practitioner coming up to you and telling you that they are sorry that X has happened. It would be better if they then also added that they are working to address the issue for you.

So, why is it wrong for healthcare practitioners to believe that saying sorry will be a problem for them? It is all down to a misunderstanding about liability and what liability means and how someone become liable.

Liability is about having duties and obligations. For instance, a healthcare practitioner has a duty of care to you (which is examined below when we discuss negligence) and an obligation to keep you safe. If a healthcare practitioner breaches their duty to you, they then are liable for that breach of duty. Liability here means that they could be subject to a sanction, such as being suspended from work or even dismissed, depending upon the severity of their breach of duty.

All healthcare practitioners have a duty of care to all of their patients. The duty exists as part of their contract of employment, and a duty will also exist as part of their registration with a healthcare regulator.

So far, so good. A healthcare practitioner has a duty of care for their patients and is expected to keep those patients safe. This is not unexpected. If they breach that duty, then they are liable for this. Again, as expected. The problem with saying sorry arises because there is a mistaken belief that liability can be transferred between people after an event has happened.

As an example, let's suppose Lindsay is a physiotherapist and during treatment on your arm she manages to sprain your wrist. She doesn't apologise but Marc, a nurse, sees what has happened and says he is sorry for the pain you are suffering. Marc was not involved in the treatment on your arm and did not cause your wrist sprain. However, some healthcare practitioners would see Marc saying sorry as him admitting that something has happened, and by acknowledging it, he now has liability for your sprained wrist.

The actual legal position is that you cannot have liability placed upon you for saying sorry. Obviously if you already had liability and you said sorry then you would continue to have liability, and this would be expected. However, where you previously had no liability, saying sorry to a patient for something that happened to them would not suddenly mean that the healthcare practitioner has assumed any liability.

The belief that liability was assumed if a healthcare practitioner said sorry was so widespread that the actual position was clarified in legislation. Section 2 of the Compensation Act 2006 states 'an apology, an offer of treatment or other redress, shall not of itself amount to an admission of negligence or breach of statutory duty'. This is a longwinded way of acknowledging that saying sorry does not equal liability.

So, if it is only an apology that is needed and that you want, there is no reason why a healthcare practitioner cannot say sorry to you.

₠ Healthcare practitioners and saying sorry

As the previous part of this section has just explained, it is a myth that if you apologise to a patient for something that has happened to them, regardless of whether you were involved or not, you are accepting liability for that event.

If something has happened to a patient and you are aware of that 'something' you should say sorry. The reasons for this are:

- It is a requirement of your regulatory body that you acknowledge any omissions on your part and apologise for them
- It is part of your professional duty of candour (see the next section for further discussion on this point)
- It is part of professional healthcare practice
- It allows the patient who is affected to know that you recognise that something has happened and that you acknowledge this, and hopefully are taking steps to rectify it

To reiterate, there is no reason why, as a healthcare practitioner, you cannot apologise for something that has happened to a patient, even if it was not your fault. Saying sorry is not an admission of liability and does not affect any liability you already have, nor does it give you liability where you did not already have it.

Duty of candour and the professional duty of candour

Although a healthcare practitioner apologising for something that has happened to a patient can be all that is needed, especially if no harm occurred to the patient, sometimes it is not enough. Where harm occurs to a patient as a result of the actions of a healthcare practitioner, there is often a need to know more about what happened, what the consequences for the patient are, and what can be done to minimise these consequences. This is where the duty of candour can come in.

A little bit of background before we discuss what the duty of candour is. The establishment of the duty of candour as a requirement in healthcare practice can be linked back to the Inquiry into the scandal into the Mid Staffordshire NHS Hospital Trust. The public inquiry was established in June 2010 and published its report in February 2013. The Inquiry was held to examine up to 1,200 deaths that occurred at Stafford Hospital between January 2005 and March 2009 that were due to poor care, abuse and neglect.

One of the findings of the Inquiry was that there was a culture of fear which led to individuals not raising their concerns, and that this in turn led to deaths continuing because of the perpetuation of the abuse, neglect and poor care.

The Inquiry recognised that to counter a culture of fear where individuals did not feel able to raise their concerns three things were needed:

- *'Openness: enabling concerns to be raised and disclosed freely without fear, and for questions to be answered;*
- *Transparency: allowing true information about performance and outcomes to be shared with staff, patients and the public;*
- *Candour: ensuring that patients harmed by a healthcare service are informed of the fact and that an appropriate remedy is offered'*

(at paragraph 1.176 of the Mid Staffordshire NHS Foundation Trust Public Inquiry Executive Summary (2013)).

As part of its recommendations, the Inquiry recognised that openness, transparency and candour were a requirement through the NHS as a whole. In response to the report of the Inquiry and its recommendations, the government announced that '*we are introducing a statutory duty of candour on all heath providers, making it a requirement for them to be open and honest where there have been failings in care*' (Department of Health 2014 at page 10).

The duty of candour came into effect in 2014 as part of The Health and Social Care Act 2008 (Regulated Activities) Regulations 2014 which made it a statutory duty.

The actual duty of candour is in regulation 20 where it states, '*a health service body must act in an open and transparent way with relevant persons in relation to care and treatment provided to service users in carrying on a regulated activity*'. What this means for patients is that if something untoward happens to them, the organisation that provides their care and treatment has a statutory duty to:

- inform the patient(s) about the incident
- as soon as possible after the incident happened
- with all the facts and information that are known
- providing support to anyone affected by the incident
- maintain a record of the incident and the actions taken afterwards
- give an apology to the patient(s) and any others affected

Effectively, the duty of candour has put what was best practice previously onto a statutory basis, so that it is a requirement for all healthcare providers. For patients it should mean that they receive the apology we discussed in the previous section, as well as an explanation and support to put right what has gone wrong as far as that is possible.

Healthcare practitioners and the professional duty of candour

The duty of candour just discussed is a statutory duty on healthcare providers, that is, on the organisations that provide healthcare. It is not a duty on individual healthcare practitioners.

However, recognising the importance of healthcare being provided in an open and transparent way by healthcare practitioners who are open, transparent and candid with their patients, the healthcare practitioner regulators issued a joint statement in 2014 where they effectively imposed a duty of candour on all the healthcare practitioners they regulate. It is known as the professional duty of candour, to distinguish it from the duty of candour that applies to healthcare providers, and it applies to all registered healthcare practitioners.

The professional duty of candour echoes that of the duty of candour. In their joint statement the healthcare practitioner regulators declared that:

> 'Every healthcare professional must be open and honest with patients when something goes wrong with their treatment or care which causes, or has the potential to cause, harm or distress.

This means that healthcare professionals must:

- *tell the patient (or, where appropriate, the patient's advocate, carer or family) when something has gone wrong;*
- *apologise to the patient (or, where appropriate, the patient's advocate, carer or family);*
- *offer an appropriate remedy or support to put matters right (if possible); and*
- *explain fully to the patient (or, where appropriate, the patient's advocate, carer or family) the short and long term effects of what has happened'*

(Chief Executives of statutory regulators of healthcare professionals 2014).

For healthcare practitioners this means that if they have made a mistake or caused an adverse event to a patient(s), they have to tell the patient about this as well as offering their apology and supporting the patient in achieving a remedy.

Complaints

You have a right to complain about the care and treatment you receive. The rest of this section will concentrate on complaints in relation to NHS healthcare because there are too many different policies and procedures relating to private healthcare providers. However, the principles we discus will have general application across all healthcare organisations.

In chapter 1 *Rights,* we discussed the difference between healthcare wishes, healthcare entitlements, and healthcare rights and how documents such as the NHS Constitution and the Patient's Charter can sometime confuse the difference between what is a right and what is an aspiration that the NHS wants to provide. We noted that whilst rights are legally enforceable, an aspiration of the NHS is not. However, just because something is not legally enforceable does not mean that you cannot complain about it if it is not delivered or is not delivered to an acceptable standard.

A complaint is essentially a way of stating that you are dissatisfied with something. A complaint can be about an individual healthcare practitioner, a group or team of healthcare practitioners, or an aspect of care or treatment. Complaints can also be informal or formal.

The difference between raising a concern and making a complaint is that with a complaint, the person making it is expecting a response to their complaint.

Reasons to complain

There are numerous reasons why a patient may want to complain about an aspect of their care or treatment. Each patient will have their own personal and unique reason why they are making their complaint. However, some common reasons for making a complaint include:

- obtaining an apology
- highlighting poor practice
- so that something that happened to one patient does not happen to another patient
- to get information about something that happened
- to get help
- to blame someone for an event that happened
- instead of going to court

As we saw in the sections on apologies and duty of candour, it should not be necessary to make a complaint in order to receive an apology or to receive information about an adverse event.

Informal and formal complaints

The difference between an informal and a formal complaint is how it is made and how it is dealt with. Informal complaints are generally made verbally, whilst a formal complaint is more usually made in writing, sometimes on a template form. A record is kept of formal complaints and the actions taken, whilst an informal complaint usually doesn't have a record kept of it. Finally, an informal complaint is dealt with locally. For instance, if an informal complaint was made to the nurse in charge of a ward it would be dealt with on the ward. A formal complaint will go through the organisation's complaint process and probably be dealt with by nominated individuals or even a specified department, depending upon the size of the organisation. This ensures consistency in dealing with complaints and that the processes are followed.

⚹ *How to make a complaint*

Most organisations will have a complaints policy and procedure, and all NHS providers are required to have their own complaints procedure. These will detail how to make a complaint and how it will be dealt with. The complaints procedure will normally include a timeframe and what you can expect at each stage of the timeframe, and what to do if you are not satisfied with the response you get. Apart from the need for consistency in dealing with complaints and providing information to those who wish to make a complaint, another reason for having a complaints policy is to ensure that complaints receive the appropriate level of attention so that more serious complaints are not dealt with informally.

If you are thinking about making a complaint about any aspect of your healthcare, it would be beneficial to obtain the relevant complaint policy from the organisation(s) who provided your care and treatment. One reason for this is that the complaints procedure will detail the time limit that you have to raise a complaint. Generally, you would have 12 months from the time you became aware of the issue.

The resources section at the back of the book has the web addresses of the NHS complaints procedures for England, Northern Ireland, Scotland and Wales.

It does not have to be the patient who makes the complaint; it can be a relative, carer or friend. If a relative, carer or friend is making the complaint, they should have the permission of the patient to do so as well as their consent to provide any confidential information that is needed.

Whilst it is possible to make an anonymous complaint, not

providing your details will mean that you will not receive a reply to your complaint. Also, making a complaint anonymously may mean that you do not provide all the relevant details, as you will not include details that identify you, and likely mean that your complaint cannot be fully investigated.

Assistance with making a complaint

Some people are uncomfortable making a complaint or do not know how best to make their complaint. There are various services available to assist people in making a complaint about the healthcare and treatment they have received.

As discussed in chapter 1 *Rights*, various advocacy services exist that patients, their relatives, and their carers can utilise. In relation to making a complaint about NHS healthcare services, the Patient Advice and Liaison Service (PALS) provides assistance to patients and others to resolve issues informally. The PALS details, including how to find the details for PALS in local NHS organisations, is in the resources section.

Where it is not possible to resolve an issue or complaint informally, the NHS Complaints Advocacy service provide advocacy to patients and other individuals who are making a complaint or thinking of making a complaint. The details for the NHS Complaints Advocacy service are also available in the resources section.

Who deals with a complaint

If your complaint involves more than one NHS organisation or provider, you do not have to make a separate complaint to each. You can make a complaint to one of the organisations and they are required to ensure that they notify all the other organisations. They must work together to address your complaint and provide a response that addresses all of the issues that you have raised.

If you make your complaint informally it should be dealt with by the individual(s) or clinical area who you raised it with if this is possible.

For a formal complaint, it is unlikely that the healthcare practitioners or clinical areas/units you have complained about will deal with your complaint. Rather, as noted earlier, there will be a manager who will deal with your complaint and correspond with you, or in very large organisations a department will handle all complaints.

If you are unsatisfied with the outcome of a complaint you have made, you can use any appeal process that the organisation has. If there is no appeal process or the outcome from that is unsatisfactory, you can take your complaint to the Parliamentary and Health Service Ombudsman. The Ombudsman acts as a final stage for complaints about NHS services and the details for the Ombudsman are in the resources section.

Complaints and your healthcare treatment

It is natural to worry that if you are currently receiving care and treatment from a healthcare practitioner or a healthcare organisation and you complain about them, that this will affect the care and treatment that you receive in the future. It shouldn't, but it may.

The reason it shouldn't affect your future care and treatment is that healthcare practitioners and organisations should approach you and your care objectively. The fact that you have made a complaint should not be detrimental to the care and treatment you receive as that has to be based on your clinical need.

That said, it may be possible that due to the nature of your complaint, the healthcare practitioner cannot continue to provide your care and treatment so that another healthcare practitioner has to take over from them. In this way, your healthcare treatment may be affected by a change in practitioner.

What should never happen is that your access to healthcare treatment is affected. You should not have a reduction in the services available to you because you have made a complaint.

You may find that your healthcare record contains relevant details of the complaint that you have made. This should not happen as a matter of routine and your healthcare record should not have a copy of your complaint attached to it along with the response to that complaint Rather, if the nature of the complaint is one that future healthcare practitioners who care and treat you need to be aware of, relevant details of the issue and the resolution may be included in your healthcare record.

⚄ Complaints as feedback

No healthcare practitioner would want to receive a complaint about their practice or the healthcare organisation they work for. However, a complaint, if taken as an indicator that something has gone wrong, or at least not gone to plan, can be used as a form of feedback. Feedback provides information that can be used to improve an aspect of practice that needs addressing.

Sometimes, it is through complaints that service improvement is achieved, and the complaint provides the information that can be acted upon to effect change. It is not the ideal method of improving practice and the service that is provided to patients, but a complaint can be an opportunity to resolve more than the actual complaint made by the patient.

Negligence

Negligence is a specific form of civil wrong which is done by one person to another. When you hear one person say they are going to sue someone else, very often they are referring to taking them to court for negligence. To sue someone means to take them to court.

If a patient has suffered harm as a result of the actions of a healthcare practitioner, they may have to sue that healthcare practitioner for negligence to seek redress. The rest of this section will discuss how a patient can prove that a healthcare practitioner was in fact negligent.

For negligence to have occurred, one person has to have a duty of care to another person. They must have breached that duty of care and in breaching it caused harm to the other person. In a healthcare setting, negligence would occur if a healthcare practitioner who owes a duty of care to a patient breached their duty to the patient by giving a poor standard of care, and the poor care resulted in the patient being harmed.

Negligence is a civil matter. This means that to bring a claim for negligence, one person has to sue another. If the harm that resulted due to the negligent act resulted in the death of the patient, this could be gross negligent manslaughter which is a criminal offence and will be tried in the criminal courts.

It is only relatively recently that negligence has existed as form of legal action. The case which established negligence was in 1932. The case was Donoghue v Stevenson [1932] and was about a woman (Mrs Donoghue) who became unwell after consuming a drink her friend had purchased for her in a cafe. Because Mrs Donoghue had not purchased the drink, she did not have a contract with the cafe and so, at the time could not take any legal action against the cafe for the illness she suffered. The judge in the case concluded that a manufacturer owes a duty of care to the ultimate consumer of a product.

You may have come across the term 'clinical negligence'. This is simply used to indicate negligence that occurs in a healthcare setting. It is not consistently used for healthcare negligence, and so we will use the term 'negligence' in the rest of our discussion to include any and all forms of negligence.

Because negligence is a civil matter, the person bringing the case, known as the claimant, has to prove their case against the defendant, the person who the claimant is saying was negligent. To prove their case the claimant has to prove 4 elements:

- that the defendant owed them a duty of care
- that the duty of care was breached
- that they suffered harm
- that the harm was caused by the breach of the duty owed to them

If the claimant fails to prove at least one of these 4 things, they will lose their case.

Negligence cases are heard before a judge. Because they are civil cases, the decision is based on the balance of probabilities. This essentially means which argument, the claimant's or the defendant's, is more probable.

We will now examine each of the 4 elements that need to be proved by a claimant in turn.

Duty of care

In most cases where the claimant is alleging that the defendant was negligent, the claimant has to prove that the defendant did in fact owe them a duty of care in the first place. This is because if there is no duty of care owed by the defendant to the claimant, then the defendant cannot be held to be negligent by them.

A duty of care means that one person has a legal obligation to another. That obligation is to act with care when dealing with the other person.

In many cases there have been extensive arguments about whether a duty of care does actually exist or not. However, in cases involving alleged healthcare negligence by a healthcare practitioner to a patient, this is usually not a matter of argument. This is because all healthcare practitioners are held to have a duty of care to their patients, and this exists under their contract of employment and through their registration with one of the healthcare practitioner regulatory bodies.

So, if a patient brings a case of alleged negligence against their healthcare practitioner, they will have already proved this point in their case. This moves the case onto the next point the patient will need to prove, which is that the healthcare practitioner breached their duty of care.

Breach of duty

In order to determine if a healthcare practitioner has breached their duty of care to a patient, it is necessary to know what standard they have to reach to fulfil their duty. Then, if they have not reached that standard, we can say that they have failed or breached their duty.

Over the years, a number of different tests have been used to determine the standard that a defendant has to reach. The standard has moved from what a reasonable person would have done in the same circumstances, to what a reasonable member of the public would expect the defendant to have done (this is often referred to as 'the man on the Clapham omnibus test'). However, given that the 'reasonable person' and 'man on the Clapham omnibus' do not necessarily know what it is reasonable to expect a healthcare practitioner to do in any given set of circumstances, a more specialised test was needed.

This arrived in 1957 as a result of the Bolam v Friern Hospital Management Committee [1957] case. The Bolam case concerned a patient, Mr Bolam, who suffered fractures of his pelvis whilst receiving electroconvulsive therapy. Mr Bolam's argument was that had the healthcare practitioner administered muscle relaxants during the therapy, the fractures would not have occurred.

It was agreed by both sides in the trial that muscle relaxants would have prevented the risk of the fractures. However, the defendant argued that there was an alternative view about the use of muscle relaxants to prevent fractures during electroconvulsive therapy. This view was that the risk of fractures was very small, and the use of a muscle relaxant carried its own risk, and so their use was not warranted.

The judge in the case, stated that

> 'where you get a situation which involves the use of some special skill or competence, then the test whether there has been negligence or not is not the test of the man on the top of a Clapham omnibus, because he has not got this special skill. The test is the standard of the ordinary skilled man exercising and professing to have that special skill. A man need not possess the highest expert skill at the risk of being found negligent. It is well established law that it is sufficient if he exercises the ordinary skill of an ordinary competent man exercising that particular art' (Bolam v Friern Hospital Management Committee [1957] at page 121).

What this means is 'what would someone with the same skills do in the same situation?'. It is similar to the reasonable man test but replaces the reasonable man with a reasonable healthcare practitioner who has the same skills as the defendant. That is, someone who understands what is needed and what should be done in the circumstances.

If the reasonable practitioner would do the same as the defendant, then the defendant will not have breached their duty of care to their patient. In the Bolam case, because there were two bodies of opinion, one to give muscle relaxants and one not to give, and the defendant did the same as one of these, he won his case.

The standard of doing what other responsible healthcare practitioners would do – having the same skills as you, and in the same circumstances, as a measure of the standard of the duty of care became known as the 'Bolam test'. Essentially, the standard is one of professional judgement and a defendant is measured against their peers. Only when their peers would disagree with the healthcare practitioner's actions would the defendant be seen to have breached the duty of care they owed to the claimant.

To determine what other responsible healthcare practitioners would do in the same set of circumstances as the defendant, expert witnesses are used to explain what it is reasonable to expect a healthcare practitioner to do.

Although the Bolam test was used for over 40 years in its original form, there were challenges to its objectivity and as a consequence in 1998 Bolitho v City & Hackney Health Authority it became modified as a result of the [1998] case. In this case, a 2-year-old boy, Patrick Bolitho, died because he was not intubated and suffered respiratory and cardiac arrest as a consequence of having croup. Using the 'Bolam test', no negligence was found because it was argued that there was a body of responsible healthcare practitioners who would not have intubated Patrick.

The outcome of the case was challenged and went to the House of Lords where it was held that

'a court is not bound to hold that a doctor can escape liability for negligence merely by producing evidence from a number of experts that his opinion accorded with medical practice. The body of opinion relied upon must have a basis in logic, and the judge must be satisfied that the experts have directed their minds to the question of comparative risks and benefits and have reached a defensible conclusion on the matter' (Bolitho v City & Hackney Health Authority [1998] at page 242).

With regard to establishing whether a healthcare practitioner has breached their duty of care, the Bolitho case means that the healthcare practitioner can no longer just rely on there being a body of responsible healthcare practitioners who would do the same as them. Instead, what the body of responsible healthcare practitioners say they would do has to withstand logical scrutiny.

It is only where an action by a healthcare practitioner is one that is based in logic can they be said to have met the standard required for their duty of care. This requirement for a logical and rational basis for any decision made by a healthcare practitioner is known as the 'Bolitho test'. It has not replaced the 'Bolam test' but has modified it so that the 'Bolam test' now requires that a healthcare practitioner acts in accordance with what other responsible healthcare practitioners, who have the same skills as the defendant, would do in the same circumstances based on a logical rationale for their actions.

Harm

Harm can refer to any form of loss that the claimant has suffered. In cases of healthcare negligence, the claimant or patient will likely have suffered some form of physical, mental or psychological trauma. If a surgeon cuts the patient's wrong leg off during an operation, then the harm will be having the good leg amputated. If a nurse gives the wrong medication to a patient and the patient has an allergic rection, the symptoms and consequences of the allergic reaction are the harm the patient has suffered.

However, harm can also be to the patient's property if the healthcare practitioner was under a duty to care for it, perhaps because the patient was unconscious or otherwise lacked the capacity to care for it themselves.

If a defendant healthcare practitioner did in fact have a duty of care to a patient, and did breach that duty, but the patient suffered no harm, no adverse effects of any form or kind, then the healthcare practitioner will not be held to be negligent because of the fact that the patient suffered no loss. This makes sense because if something happens, but you suffer no harm or loss and you bring a case against someone, what actually are you claiming, and what do you want to be the outcome of the case?

The breach caused the harm

Looking at how the healthcare practitioner's breach of the duty of care they owed to their patient caused the harm that the patient suffered is known as causation.

To win their case, the claimant has to prove what is known as factual causation, which asks a simple question that can be very difficult to answer. That question is, but for the actions of the defendant, would the claimant's harm have occurred? The crucial part of the question is 'but for'.

Factual causation is seeking to establish whether the defendant, by breaching their duty of care to the claimant, caused the harm the claimant suffered. Lord Denning gave a useful explanation of how to use the 'but for' test when he stated that

> '*if you can say that the damage would not have happened BUT FOR a particular fault, then that fault is in fact the cause of the damage; but if you can say that the damage would have happened just the same, fault or no fault, then the fault is not the cause of the damage*' (Cork v Kirby Maclean Ltd [1952] at page 407).

In his statement, the fault Lord Denning is referring to is the breach of the duty of care. Therefore, if a patient would not have suffered harm *but for* the actions of the healthcare practitioner, then factual causation will have been proved. If, however, something else could have caused the harm suffered by the patient or the harm would have occurred regardless of the healthcare practitioner's breach of duty to their patient, then factual causation will not be proved, and the claimant will lose their case.

Assuming that the claimant has proved each of the preceding three points, if factual causation is proved the case moves on to consider what outcome the claimant should achieve by winning their case.

Outcome in negligence cases

Not being able to prove that the defendant owed them a duty of care and subsequently breached this duty, causing harm to the claimant would mean that the claimant loses their case and the defendant wins.

If the claimant is able to prove each of the four points required, they will have won their case and the case then turns to look at what the claimant has won.

The outcome of a negligence case is damages. This is a monetary award that compensates the patient for the harm they have suffered. The money is intended to put the patient in the position they would have been in had the harm not occurred. If the patient was previously employed but because of the harm suffered, they are no longer able to work, then the damages will replace actual and future lost earnings. If the patient is unable to walk because of the harm they suffered, the damages will be intended to assist them in any adaptations they need to their home and to assist their mobility, for example with a car adapted to their needs. If a patient needs 24-hour nursing care because of the harm they suffered, the damages will pay for that nursing care. In addition to the damages, to put the patient in the position they would have been in had the harm not occurred, an amount of damages may be awarded to compensate the patient for the pain and suffering they have endured as a result of the harm.

However, a claimant should not expect an apology or an

explanation of how the harm occurred as a result of winning a negligence case. This may happen, but it is not part of the outcome.

▣ Team liability and the standard for student and trainee healthcare practitioners

There is no legal concept of team liability and if a healthcare practitioner is part of a team when they breach their duty of care to a patient, they cannot use the fact that they were part of a team as their defence to a negligence action against them. Rather, each member of the team is responsible for demonstrating that their actions met the requirements of the modified 'Bolam test' as discussed above.

If the healthcare practitioner who is alleged to have breached their duty of care is a trainee or a student, this does not mean that a different test is used to determine if they have met the required standard. The test remains the modified 'Bolam test'. What does change is who is considered to be the body of responsible healthcare practitioners.

In all cases where the modified 'Bolam test' is used, the body of responsible healthcare practitioners is the defendant's peers. So, if the defendant is a trainee or student, then the body of responsible healthcare practitioners would be trainees and students and it is against their actions that the defendant would be judged. Similarly, if the defendant was an advanced practitioner, then their actions would be judged against a body of responsible advanced healthcare practitioners.

Regulation of healthcare practitioners

In this section we are going to examine how healthcare practitioners are regulated. That is, how their practice is overseen, and what a patient can do if they have a concern about a healthcare practitioner's practice.

Healthcare practitioner regulators

A regulator is an organisation that can control or limit a particular activity or role or function. The healthcare practitioner regulators are able to control who is admitted to the registers they maintain and therefore who is able to work as a registered healthcare practitioner.

There are several healthcare practitioner regulators who each maintain a register for a defined group(s) of healthcare practitioner(s). These regulators and the healthcare practitioners they regulate are:

- Health and Care Professions Council – arts therapists, biomedical scientists, chiropodists and podiatrists, clinical scientists, dietitians, hearing aid dispensers, occupational therapists, operating department practitioners, orthoptists, paramedics, physiotherapists, practitioner psychologists, prosthetists and orthotists, radiographers, and speech and language therapists
- General Chiropractic Council – chiropractors
- General Dental Council – dentists and other dental care practitioners including dental nurses and hygienists
- General Medical Council – doctors
- General Optical Council – optometrists and dispensing opticians
- General Osteopathic Council – osteopaths
- General Pharmaceutical Council (in Northern Ireland the regulator is the Pharmaceutical Society of Northern Ireland) – pharmacists and pharmacy technicians
- Nursing & Midwifery Council – midwives, nurses and nursing associates

The main focus of the healthcare practitioner regulators is to promote patient safety and protect the public. They do this by regulating healthcare practitioners through five main mechanisms, these being:

- setting the standards for entry to the register
- establishing the training and education requirement for initial entry to the register
- maintaining a register of healthcare practitioners who have met the required standard for entry and restricting entry to only those who have met the standard
- setting the standard for maintaining registration, both in terms of the healthcare practitioner's competence and their adherence to the code of conduct the regulator produces
- investigating the fitness to practise of those on the register if there is any reason to suspect that they are not performing at the required standard, and removing those who fail to meet the required standard from the register

The healthcare practitioner regulators all have statutory authority to act as a regulator, their role and function being set out in the legislation that established them. As they all have a common function there is considerable overlap in their role and how they approach it, although there are also differences between them and the requirements they set for their respective registrant healthcare practitioners.

It is the registered healthcare practitioners who pay for the healthcare practitioner regulator's costs through a registration fee that is paid on initial registration and then at periodic intervals – usually annually or every two or three years.

If a healthcare practitioner is not registered with the relevant regulator for their role, they will not be able to undertake that role. For instance, if a nurse is not registered with the Nursing & Midwifery Council, they will not be able to take on the role of a registered nurse.

The standard required of healthcare practitioners

The healthcare practitioner regulators set the initial standard that healthcare practitioners have to meet to gain entry to the register and also the standard that healthcare practitioners have to meet to maintain their registration. There are two main aspects to the standard required for healthcare practitioners to maintain their registration with a regulator. These are competence, and adherence to the regulator's code of conduct.

Competence here refers to the ability of a healthcare practitioner to perform their role. It is a reflection of the healthcare practitioner's abilities, knowledge and skills. It is a requirement of continued registration with a regulator that healthcare practitioners maintain their competence. If a healthcare practitioner wishes to take on additional roles or advance their practice, they have to achieve competence in that role before they are able to do it unsupervised.

In order to maintain their competence, healthcare practitioners are required to demonstrate that they have undertaken a set level of continuing professional development. The amount of continuing professional development and the period over which it has to be achieved varies from regulator to regulator.

Some of the regulators, for instance the General Medical Council and the Nursing & Midwifery Council, require the healthcare practitioners on their registers to undergo revalidation. This is a process whereby every few years, the healthcare practitioner has to demonstrate that they are competent to continue to practise as a registered practitioner. Amongst other conditions, it requires the healthcare practitioner to show they have achieved a set number of hours of practice, a set number of hours of professional development, and that they meet the health and character requirements of the regulator.

One of the main requirements for healthcare practitioners is that they do not practise outside of their level of competence.

Doing so would mean that they are not meeting the required standard and so could face an investigation into their practice.

The healthcare practitioner regulators inform the healthcare practitioners on their registers of the standards that they expect them to reach via the codes of conduct they issue. Each of the healthcare practitioner regulators has different names for their codes of conduct. For example, the General Medical Council's code is called *Good medical practice*, whilst that from the Health and Care Professions Council is called *Standards of conduct, performance and ethics* and that from the Nursing & Midwifery Council is *The code: professional standards of practice and behaviour for nurses, midwives and nursing associates*.

Failure by healthcare practitioners to adhere to the principles in their respective codes of conduct can be reason for them to have their fitness to practise investigated by their regulator.

ℛ *Raising a concern with a healthcare practitioner regulator*

If you have a concern about a healthcare practitioner's practice or their ability to undertake their practice, you can raise a concern with their regulator. All of the regulators have a similar process for raising a concern with them and their websites detail the ways that this can be done. The website addresses of each of the regulators are included in the resources section. There are sources of help available to patients and members of the public in raising a concern, but concerns can also be made by employers and colleagues of the healthcare practitioner.

The role of the healthcare practitioner regulators is to protect the public and maintain patient safety by only allowing competent healthcare practitioners to practise within their area of remit. Therefore, if a concern is raised with them or they otherwise come to know about a possible area of concern, they can investigate the practice of the relevant healthcare practitioner(s). This is known as a fitness to practise investigation.

The healthcare practitioner regulators have a wide remit of areas of concern that they can investigate. These include allegations, violence by healthcare practitioners to patients or others, breaches of confidentiality, dishonesty, poor practice and when the healthcare practitioner has committed a criminal offence.

However, the healthcare practitioner regulators are only able to investigate a healthcare practitioner if they are on the register they hold. Therefore, a concern needs to be raised with the correct regulator.

The purpose of a fitness to practise investigation is to determine if there are grounds for proceeding to a fitness to practise hearing.

A fitness to practise hearing will hear the concern that has been raised, any evidence that has been submitted, and will ask witnesses to attend so that they can be questioned. The healthcare practitioner is entitled to be represented and can challenge the evidence that is presented and question witnesses, usually through their representative. The hearing is conducted according to the civil justice rules and the decision is made on the balance of probabilities.

Fitness to practise hearings are generally held in public, so it is possible to attend a hearing if you have raised a concern. However, there may be rules about not attending until after you have given your evidence if you have been called to give evidence. Once the hearing has considered all the evidence, they will reach a decision as to whether the healthcare practitioner's fitness to practise is impaired. The healthcare practitioner will be judged according to the relevant code of conduct and whether there is evidence that they breached the principles in the code or not. If it is not, then the healthcare practitioner will be free to continue to practise. If it is found that the healthcare practitioner has impaired practice, the hearing will move on to consider the sanction that should be applied to their practice. The sanctions available to a fitness to practise hearing are discussed below.

In considering what sanction should be applied to the healthcare practitioner's practice, the hearing will consider whether there is any extenuating or mitigating factors that could lessen the sanctions that are applied. This could be that the healthcare practitioner is aware that they have fallen below the required standard and has taken steps to improve their practice and learn from the incident(s).

The hearing will also consider where there are any factors that call for a more severe sanction to be applied such as the healthcare practitioner not having any insight into their actions and why they are falling short of the required standard as outlined in the code of conduct. Other considerations that the hearing will take into account are whether the issue was a one-off event or is part of a series of failings, the seriousness of the issue(s), and whether it resulted in any harm to anyone.

The sanction that is applied has to be proportionate to the seriousness of the healthcare practitioner's failing. However, it also has to be sufficient to protect patients and allow the public to have faith in the ability of healthcare practitioner regulators to regulate healthcare practitioners and protect them from those who do not practise to a sufficient standard.

A healthcare practitioner is able to appeal a decision that is made by a fitness to practise hearing, either on the basis of the severity of the sanction that they have been given or on the basis of the finding itself. It is also possible for the Professional Standards Authority, which oversees the work of the healthcare practitioner regulators, to challenge a sanction for being too lenient or to challenge the decision that has been made.

The Professional Standards Authority acts as a safeguard for the public and patients that the correct decision has been made and that the appropriate sanction has been applied.

Sanctions available to healthcare practitioner regulators

Although the different healthcare practitioner regulators use different terminology, they all have the same range of sanctions available to them for healthcare practitioners whose practice has been found to be below the required standard so that their fitness to practise is impaired.

These sanctions range from:

- issuing a warning or a reprimand to the healthcare practitioner that they need to improve their practice
- putting a condition on the healthcare practitioner's practice, so that they can only undertake their practice if they comply with the conditions. For instance, only working under supervision or only being able to issue medicine after doing a retraining course.
- suspending the healthcare practitioner from practising for periods up to 12 months
- permanently removing the healthcare practitioner from the register so that they cannot practise as a healthcare practitioner in any of the areas covered by that regulator.

If a healthcare practitioner regulator sanctions a healthcare practitioner because of a concern you have raised with them, the sanction that they impose will be the end of the matter. They cannot order the healthcare practitioner to apologise to you or provide any explanation.

REFERENCES

Abortion Act 1967

Airedale NHS Trust v Bland [1993] 1 All ER 821

Bolam v Friern Hospital Management Committee [1957] 2 All ER 118

Bolitho v City & Hackney Health Authority [1998]

Carers UK (n.d.) *Why we're here* Available at https://www.carersuk. org/about-us/why-were-here/

Chatterton v. Gerson [1981] 1 All ER 257

Chief Executives of statutory regulators of healthcare professionals (2014) *Openness and honesty – the professional duty of candour* available at: https://www.gcc-uk.org/assets/publications/Joint_statement_on_the_professional_duty_of_candour.pdf

Children Act 1989

Compensation Act 2006

Cork v Kirby Maclean Ltd [1952] 2 All ER 402

Coroners and Justice Act 2009

Crown Prosecution Service (2014) *Suicide: Policy for Prosecutors in Respect of Cases of Encouraging or Assisting Suicide*: Available at: www.cps.gov.uk/legal-guidance/suicide-policy- prosecutors-respect-cases-encouraging-or-assisting-suicide

Data Protection Act 2018

Department of Health (1991) *The Patient's Charter* Department of Health, London

Department of Health (2014) *Hard truths: The journey to putting patients first* Cm-8777-I and Cm 8711-II Department of Health, London

Department of Health and Social Care (2021) *NHS Constitution for England* available at https://www.gov.uk/government/publications/the-nhs-constitution-for-england/the-nhs-constitution-for-england

Family Law Reform Act 1969

F v West Berkshire Health Authority [1989] 2 ALL ER 545

General Medical Council (2020) *Good medical practice* General Medical Council, London

Health and Care Professions Council (2016) *Standards of conduct, performance and ethics* Health and Care Professions Council, London

Human Fertilisation and Embryology Act 1990

Human Rights Act 1998

Human Tissue Act 2004

Interpretation Act 1850

Mental Capacity Act 2005

Mental Health Act 1983

Mid Staffordshire NHS Foundation Trust Public Inquiry. (2013). *Report of the Mid Staffordshire NHS Foundation Trust Public Inquiry: Executive summary (HC 947). The Stationery Office, London.*

Montgomery v Lanarkshire Health Board [2015] UKSC 11

Nursing and Midwifery Council (2018) *The Code* Nursing and Midwifery Council, London

Re B (adult: refusal of medical treatment) [2002] 2 All ER 449

Re T (Adult: refusal of medical treatment) [1992] 4 All ER 649

Stevenson A (ed) (2007) *Shorter Oxford English Dictionary* 6th edition Oxford University Press, Oxford

Suicide Act 1961

Support After Suicide Partnership (2023) *Glossary* available at https://hub.supportaftersuicide.org.uk/glossary/

The Health and Social Care Act 2008 (Regulated Activities) Regulations 2014

GLOSSARY

Acts of Parliament are primary legislation. They are made in Parliament and are a way of creating a new law or modifying an existing law.

Advance decisions are a decision made by a patient in advance of an event happening. An example would be an advance directive.

Advocacy refers to acting on behalf of someone who is unable to act for themselves.

Best interests is an objective test to determine what decision on treatment would be best for this particular patient.

Brainstem death refers to the absence of reflexes from the brain via the brain stem to the spinal cord. It is one of the legal ways of determining death in the United Kingdom.

Carer is someone who provides care to a patient but does so in an unpaid capacity and without whom the patient would not be able to manage their daily life.

Chaperone is someone who acts as an impartial observer during the time a patient is having an intimate examination. Generally, a healthcare practitioner.

Child is legally defined in the Children Act 1989, section 108, as someone under the age of 18.

Common law refers to law that is based on the judgments made in cases that come before the courts and are developed over a number of years.

Competence can refer to the obligation on a healthcare practitioner to ensure that they have the necessary skills, knowledge and ability to perform their role. Or, to someone who has the ability to make their own decisions about treatment and to give their consent.

Confidentiality is about keeping information private and not sharing personal information without a lawful reason.

Conscientious objection refers to when healthcare practitioners exert their autonomy to practise according to their conscience and beliefs.

Consent refers to permission granted by one person for another person to do something. In healthcare there are specific requirements which have to be met for consent to be legally valid.

Duty of candour refers to acting with honesty and transparency, particularly when things go wrong. It only applies to healthcare providers.

Duty of care is an obligation that a healthcare practitioner has to their patient to treat them according to a given standard.

Ethics is concerned with the rules of conduct and duty that define how individuals behave toward each other.

Euthanasia literally means a *good death,* but refers to when one person ends the life of another at the first person's request.

Fitness to practise refers to whether a healthcare practitioner is meeting the standards required of them by their regulatory body.

Healthcare practitioner is a person who has skills and knowledge to assist patients in meeting their healthcare needs and is paid to do this.

Incompetent adult is a legal term that means someone who does not have the ability to make their own treatment decisions.

Lasting power of attorney is a legal authority from one person (known as the donor) to another person (known as the attorney) that allows the attorney to make decisions on behalf of the donor.

Law refers to a formal set of rules, the breaking of which can result in punishment of some sort.

Negligence is a specific form of civil wrong which is done by one person to another. If someone causes you harm, you can sue them for negligence.

Next of kin is the person you want to be contacted about your admission to hospital, or other healthcare setting, or to be kept informed about your care and treatment.

Parental responsibility refers to the rights and obligations that a person has in relation to a child. It allows a parent to make healthcare decision for a child.

Patient refers to someone who has healthcare needs.

Principle of necessity is a legal doctrine that allows healthcare practitioners to act to provide care and treatment when the patient lacks capacity.

Professional duty of candour applies to healthcare practitioners and requires them to be open and honest with their patients, particularly when something goes wrong.

Regulation is concerned with controlling or limiting a particular activity or role or function.

Relative is someone who is connected to you either though a blood line or by an affinity.

Statute is another term for an Act of Parliament.

Statutory instruments are a way of modifying existing law or certain new law without the need for an Act of Parliament. They are generally quicker to enact than an Act of Parliament.

Treatment is shorthand to mean all forms of healthcare including investigations, procedures and treatment, in fact anything that is provided by healthcare practitioners to meet a patient's healthcare needs.

Whistleblowing refers to a legal mechanism for raising a concern that provides protection to the person raising the concern, provided they meet certain criteria.

RESOURCES

These resources are the ones mentioned within the book and others that may be useful if you wish to follow up on some of the services we mention that are available to patients and carers in the different chapters.

They are arranged according to the chapter in which they are discussed.

CHAPTER 1: RIGHTS

Advocacy

Independent Mental Capacity Advocates (ICMAs) government website – https://www.gov.uk/government/publications/independent-mental-capacity-advocates

MIND how to find an advocate website – https://www.mind.org.uk/information-support/guides-to-support-and-services/advocacy/finding-an-advocate/

MIND Independent Mental Capacity Advocates (IMCA) information – https://www.mind.org.uk/information-support/guides-to-support-and-services/advocacy/imcas/

MIND Independent Mental Health Advocates (IMHA) information for England – https://www.mind.org.uk/information-support/guides-to-support-and-services/advocacy/imhas-england/

MIND Independent Mental Health Advocates (IMHA) information for Wales – https://www.mind.org.uk/information-support/guides-to-support-and-services/advocacy/imhas-wales/

NHS advocacy information – https://www.nhs.uk/conditions/social-care-and-support-guide/help-from-social-services-and-charities/someone-to-speak-up-for-you-advocate/

NHS Complaints advocacy – https://www.pohwer.net/nhs-complaints-advocacy

POhWER advocacy information and resources – https://www.pohwer.net/

The Advocacy People website – https://www.theadvocacypeople.org.uk/

Main NHS websites
NHS in England – https://www.nhs.uk/
NHS in Northern Ireland – https://online.hscni.net/
NHS in Scotland – https://www.healthscotland.scot/
NHS in Wales – https://www.nhs.wales/

CHAPTER 2: ENGAGING WITH HEALTHCARE

Carers UK website – https://www.carersuk.org/

CHAPTER 5: WHEN THE PATIENT LACKS THE CAPACITY TO CONSENT FOR THEIR OWN HEALTHCARE NEEDS

Deprivation of liberty safeguards (DoLS), government resources site – https://www.gov.uk/government/publications/deprivation-of-liberty-safeguards-forms-and-guidance
Lasting Power of Attorney (LPAs), government website with information and also to make an LPA – https://www.gov.uk/power-of-attorney
Liberty Protection Safeguards (LPS) – government information website – https://www.gov.uk/government/publications/liberty-protection-safeguards-factsheets/liberty-protection-safeguards-what-they-are

CHAPTER 7: DECISION-MAKING AROUND THE END OF LIFE

Do not attempt cardio-pulmonary resuscitation recommendation (DNACPR) – https://www.nhs.uk/conditions/do-not-attempt-cardiopulmonary-resuscitation-dnacpr-decisions/
Organ donation information – https://www.organdonation.nhs.uk/
The Support After Suicide Partnership - https://supportaftersuicide.org.uk/
TellUsOnce government service – https://www.gov.uk/after-a-death/organisations-you-need-to-contact-and-tell-us-once

CHAPTER 8: QUESTIONING HEALTHCARE

Guides to NHS complaints

England – https://www.nhs.uk/using-the-nhs/about-the-nhs/how-to-complain-to-the-nhs/

Northern Ireland – https://www.nidirect.gov.uk/articles/raising-concern-or-making-complaint-about-health-services

Scotland – https://nhsnss.org/contact-us/complaints/

Wales – https://www.wales.nhs.uk/ourservices/contactus/nhscomplaints

NHS Complaints advocacy – https://www.pohwer.net/nhs-complaints-advocacy

Parliamentary and Health Service Ombudsman – https://www.ombudsman.org.uk/

Patient Advice and Liaison Service (PALS) – https://www.nhs.uk/nhs-services/hospitals/what-is-pals-patient-advice-and-liaison-service/

Healthcare practitioner regulator websites

General Chiropractic Council – https://www.gcc-uk.org/

General Dental Council – https://www.gdc-uk.org/

General Medical Council – https://www.gmc-uk.org/

General Optical Council – https://optical.org/

General Osteopathic Council – https://www.osteopathy.org.uk/home/

General Pharmaceutical Council – https://www.pharmacyregulation.org/

Health and Care Professions Council – https://www.hcpc-uk.org/

Nursing and Midwifery Council – https://www.nmc.org.uk/

Pharmaceutical Society of Northern Ireland – https://www.psni.org.uk/

Regulation oversight body

Professional Standards Authority – https://www.professionalstandards.org.uk/home

INDEX